That's the Way I Think

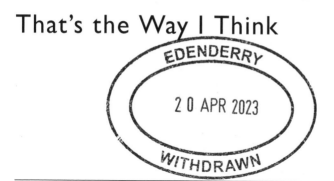

About 1 in 20 individuals are dyslexic. This figure also applies for dyspraxia and ADHD. This fully revised edition of David Grant's thought-provoking, insightful book develops our understanding of these specific learning differences and considers the further challenges presented by these overlapping conditions.

This latest edition includes a brand-new chapter on dyscalculia. Revised sections also explore updates in the study of dyslexia, dyspraxia and ADHD as well as visualisation and synaesthesia, in the light of new data and research. These updates enable the reader to gain a fuller understanding of the sensory experiences and thoughts of individuals with specific learning differences.

The author takes a life-style approach to explain many of the everyday experiences and choices of individuals with specific learning differences, including sleep, sports, visualisation and creativity, and uses real life examples explained in the words of those with specific learning differences.

The accessible style of this book will immediately strike a chord with anyone with first- or second-hand experience of specific learning differences. It is invaluable and insightful reading for those with specific learning differences as well as their parents and/or partner, teachers, teaching assistants and SENCos.

David Grant is an Associate Fellow of the British Psychological Society and was formally recognised as an Educational Psychologist by the Health Care & Professions Council in 2012.

That's the Way I Think

Dyslexia, dyspraxia, ADHD and dyscalculia explained

Third Edition

David Grant

With illustrations by
Hannah Evelyn French

Routledge
Taylor & Francis Group

LONDON AND NEW YORK

Third edition published 2017
by Routledge
2 Park Square, Milton Park, Abingdon, Oxon OX14 4RN

and by Routledge
711 Third Avenue, New York, NY 10017

Routledge is an imprint of the Taylor & Francis Group, an informa business

First edition published by David Fulton Publishers 2005
Second edition published by Routledge 2010

British Library Cataloguing in Publication Data
A catalogue record for this book is available from the British Library

Library of Congress Cataloging in Publication Data
Names: Grant, David.
Title: That's the way I think : dyslexia, dyspraxia, ADHD and
dyscalculia explained / David Grant.
Description: 3rd Edition. | New York : Routledge, 2017. | Previous
edition: 2010. | Includes bibliographical references and index.
Identifiers: LCCN 2016032529 (print) | LCCN 2016033085 (ebook) |
ISBN 9781138126213 (hardback) | ISBN 9781138126220 (paperback)
| ISBN 9781315647005 (ebk) | ISBN 9781315647005 (ebook)
Subjects: LCSH: Dyslexia. | Apraxia. | Attention-deficit hyperactivity
disorder.
Classification: LCC RC394.W6 G73 2017 (print) | LCC RC394.W6
(ebook) | DDC 616.85/53--dc23
LC record available at https://lccn.loc.gov/2016032529

ISBN: 978-1-138-12621-3 (hbk)
ISBN: 978-1-138-12622-0 (pbk)
ISBN: 978-1-315-64700-5 (ebk)

Typeset in Goudy
by HWA Text and Data Management, London

Contents

Preface

In the UK alone there are over 3 million people who are dyslexic, and the numbers are similar for both dyspraxia and attention deficit hyperactivity disorder (ADHD). Irrespective of gender or country of birth, about 1 in 20 of the population will be dyslexic, dyspraxic or have ADHD. In many countries there is a culture of shame and embarrassment associated with being diagnosed as having one of these specific learning differences. However, even when social acceptance is greater, there is frequently misunderstanding about what it actually means to be dyslexic, dyspraxic or to have ADHD. In the UK we speak of 'specific learning difficulties' and in the US 'learning disorder' is the preferred term. Both of these have negative connotations. I prefer 'specific learning difference'. Given the right set of circumstances, individuals with different ways of learning and thinking can be very successful. However, if they are required to learn and think like neurotypicals, then the result can be underperformance, failure and acute stress.

This book has been written in an informal style, using the voices and personal experiences of many to help dispel

myths and ignorance. It is a book for dipping into. It
has been written to inform not just those with a specific
learning difference, but also partners, parents, brothers and
sisters, teachers and employers, and helps to give an insight
into not only what these specific learning differences are
but also how they influence and shape so many facets of
everyday life. It is about moving beyond misunderstanding
to positivity. About six years ago I received an email from
an Egyptian woman who had bought a copy of my book
in Beirut. I have never forgotten her opening sentence,
'Your book saved my life'. When there is still so much
misunderstanding blighting the lives of so many there is
a need for a new edition drawing upon recent research
and policy changes. While the format is similar to that
of previous editions, I have chosen to completely re-
write the book, drawing upon the words and experiences
of individuals I have spent time with since the previous
edition. As a consequence, about 95 per cent of the text
is new. The scope has also been expanded to now include
discussion of dyscalculia and specific language impairment.

Acknowledgements

This book could not have been written without the conversations I have had with several thousand individuals I have assessed for specific learning differences who have shared with me their thoughts, ideas and experiences. I am also very grateful for the feedback I have received about their success and also for comments from partners and parents. To all a big thank you.

I am very pleased Hannah French has supplied four new illustrations for this edition. When I first met Hannah she was a student of Illustration at Kingston University. The combination of being dyslexic and a very creative illustrator meant the illustrations Hannah drew for the first edition captured beautifully a range of everyday dyslexic-type experiences. Since graduating Hannah has successfully completed a PGCE and an MSc. She is currently Head of an Art Department in a secondary school.

Thanks are also due to Tania, a Ravensbourne College Animation student who graduated in the summer of 2009. She is dyspraxic and has ADHD. She is also a synaesthete. Her two illustrations (10.2 and 11.1) compellingly depict her own experiences at school and with sleep.

Finally, this book is much better for being rigorously copy-edited by my wife. When I was a lecturer I advised my students to avoid letting their egos get in the way of good writing. Cathy made sure that what I meant to say was what I had written. This was not always easy – but it was essential. So thank you.

David Grant

Introduction

Prior to writing the first edition of this book in 2005 I had carried out assessments for and diagnosed about 1,000 individuals who were dyslexic, dyspraxic or both. I had learnt from them something academic textbooks did not consider – being dyslexic or dyspraxic is so much more than just difficulties with reading or motor coordination. It is a lifestyle. It affects relationships with parents and friends because, if you are dyslexic or dyspraxic, you frequently forget to do things and they don't understand why. You don't know why either, and this erodes self-confidence. It affects behaviour in class or at work, as you have to ask for things to be repeated. It influences which subjects you choose to specialise in studying and this affects the career path you follow. It impacts on sleep. It is not something you can opt in and out of. Soon after I became a Specialist Assessor I received an email that summed up this lifestyle approach. Joan described being dyslexic as 'something that is with me from the moment I wake up until the time I go to bed'. You don't have dyslexia, you are dyslexic. It is not an add-on. It is a fundamental part of who you are.

Over the years I have learnt much more about ADHD (Attention Deficit Hyperactivity Disorder) and the scope of the second edition was widened to encompass this. More recently I have been learning about dyscalculia, which is probably even more misunderstood than dyslexia, dyspraxia or ADHD. Irrespective of which specific learning difference is present, it is integral to who you are and how you experience the everyday world. In seeking to capture these everyday experiences I have chosen to write more in an oral history style than an academic one, using personal accounts and comments to illustrate points wherever possible. Care has been taken throughout to use pseudonyms and change some personal details. However, there is a universality to many of the comments.

The decision to avoid an academic style of writing was hugely driven by the fact that most academic texts are very dense and technical, and not user-friendly for those who are wanting to learn more about themselves. However, underpinning the ideas and concepts I explore in this book is an academic foundation. On those occasions when I engage in 'thinking outside the box' I have tried to make this obvious. However, it has also been necessary to challenge myths, such as ADHD being mainly a male behaviour. For this reason I have taken care to ensure the voices of women are well represented throughout the book.

In spite of what appears to be a large literature on these specific learning differences, either in print or digital form, there is still a lack of understanding and lack of recognition, with the consequence that about 90 per cent of the individuals I have assessed, who range in age from

16 to 80+, have had no previous diagnosis. In spite of the excellent work undertaken by charitable organisations, which has had a positive influence on both public and political opinion, there is still much that remains to be done. Lack of understanding results in under-achievement and personal suffering. An Amazon reviewer of a previous edition of this book wrote: 'At last, I have some understanding of why I am like I am, and can now start living with myself with less anxiety'. That is a key reason for writing this third edition.

Chapter 1

Dyslexia, dyspraxia and ADHD – the common ground

If someone has a history of difficulties with reading words with accuracy and with reading fluently, it may be because they are dyslexic. If there is a history of clumsiness or poor motor coordination, the diagnosis is likely to be one of dyspraxia (also known as Developmental Coordination Disorder). When there is a history of poor concentration, restlessness and impulsivity, the diagnosis may well be ADHD (Attention Deficit Hyperactivity Disorder). On the face of it, these three specific learning differences appear to be very different from each other, and this is true in terms of their core defining features. In the case of dyscalculia, the core defining feature is a lack of numerosity, i.e. an inability to understand the concept of 'more than/less than'. However, while dyslexia, dyspraxia and ADHD all have some key characteristics in common, dyscalculia is very different. In order to understand the everyday experiences and preferences of individuals who have dyslexia, dyspraxia or ADHD, it is necessary to understand this shared commonality, for it is fundamental in influencing and shaping the lives of these individuals.

Whenever I carry out a diagnostic assessment I begin by taking a detailed life history and then administer a range of tests. These tests fall into two general categories – providing measures of educational achievement and measures of neurocognitive function. (NB: The word 'neurocognitive' refers to mental processes which take place in the brain, such as the ability to remember and retrieve information.) By taking an individual through psychometric tests designed to measure the four areas of verbal reasoning, visual reasoning, working memory, and processing speed, a profile of neurocognitive function can be created. In general, when a neurotypical individual (i.e. someone with no known specific learning difference) takes these tests the profile of scores is quite flat. That is, there is relatively little variation in performance across these four ability sets.

However, when dyslexia, dyspraxia or ADHD is present, an individual will, in most cases, perform noticeably better on tests of verbal and visual ability than on ones of working memory and processing speed. This commonality of neurocognitive strengths and weaknesses has wide-ranging consequences for how people with dyslexia, dyspraxia and ADHD experience the world, and it influences many choices they make, including career paths and sporting preferences.

The battery of tests used internationally by psychologists such as myself to measure these four sets of abilities is known as the WAIS-IV (Wechsler Adult Intelligence Scale, 4th edition). For assessing children below the age of sixteen an equivalent battery of tests known as the WISC (Wechsler Intelligence Scale for Children), now into its fifth edition, is used. Both consist of ten core tests, five of which measure language-based abilities (Verbal

Comprehension and Working Memory) and five measure visual-based abilities (Perceptual Reasoning and Processing Speed). The ten test scores are used to calculate Index figures for the four ability sets. When the four Index figures are displayed in bar chart form, it is very easy to see whether a profile is an uneven, spiky one, as well as the degree of spikiness. The degree of an individual's cognitive strengths and weaknesses is then clearly evident.

I have used this method to illustrate the neurocognitive profiles discussed throughout this book. The greater the spikiness, the greater the severity of the specific learning difference. However, it is important to note that dyslexia, dyspraxia and ADHD are not clear-cut categories. Each has a spectrum, and the decision as to whether a specific learning difference is present is a clinical judgement rather than a statistical one. While the degree of spikiness in an individual's profile is helpful in deciding whether a specific learning difference is present, and, if so, the extent of severity (mild, moderate, severe), it also needs to be considered in the context of that person's personal history and what is required of them in their academic, work or family life. It is quite possible to be successful in one form of employment or education but then struggle in a different context. This neurocognitive profile also serves as a point of comparison with performance on tests of educational abilities, such as reading, spelling, handwriting speed and maths.

Rosanna was first diagnosed as being dyslexic in primary school. As her university needed confirmation of her early diagnosis I saw her just before she became an undergraduate.

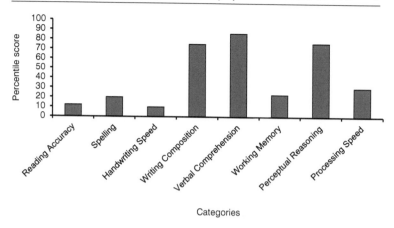

Figure 1.1 Rosanna's profile – a typical dyslexic profile

Her profile (see Figure 1.1) is a characteristic dyslexic one. As expected, her word reading accuracy, spelling ability and her speed of writing are weak. In contrast, when given a creative writing exercise, the quality of her story was very good. Rosanna performed much better on tests of verbal and visual reasoning ability than on ones of working memory and processing speed. Her spiky neurocognitive profile is typical of many dyslexic individuals.

Andre was first diagnosed as being dyspraxic when he was a business studies undergraduate. His test profile (See Figure 1.2) is a typical dyspraxic one. Unlike Rosanna, his word reading and spelling abilities are good. However, as with Rosanna, his handwriting speed is quite slow. Andre's neurocognitive profile is similar in that it also reveals a weak working memory and a slow processing speed. However, as is typical of many dyspraxics, he performed better on tests of verbal than visual reasoning. For example, an individual who is dyspraxic may have an

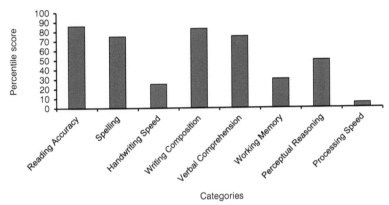

Figure 1.2 Andre's profile – a typical dyspraxic profile

excellent understanding of vocabulary but have difficulty mentally rotating shapes.

Leon was an MBA student I diagnosed as having ADHD. As would be anticipated for an MBA student, his test scores for verbal and visual reasoning are very high. However, like Rosanna and Andre, he also performed noticeably less well on tests of working memory and processing speed. Once again, his speed of writing is below expectation.

The double deficit that is such a distinctive feature of the neurocognitive profiles of Rosanna, Andre and Leon is frequently found in cases of dyslexia, dyspraxia and ADHD, irrespective of the intellectual ability, gender, ethnicity or age of the individual. However, it is not inevitably present, and there are variations on it. As a generalisation, an uneven, spiky profile is highly indicative of the presence of a specific learning difference whereas a fairly flat profile would suggest there is no specific learning difference. This is because the tests have been designed so that neurotypical individuals with no specific learning

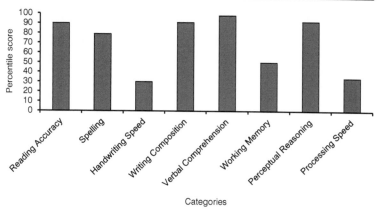

Categories

Figure 1.3 Leon's profile – a typical ADHD profile

difference who score *x* on one test are likely to score *x*, or very close to *x*, on all the other tests.

One way of understanding these four sets of neurocognitive functions is to think of your brain as being like a computer. It is as if verbal reasoning is your word processing package (this includes the dictionary and thesaurus), working memory is RAM (Random Access Memory), perceptual reasoning is the graphics card, and processing speed is the processing chip – how fast you can transmit information from eye to hand and how quickly you can visually scan and process information. In the cases of Rosanna, Andre and Leon, they are all capable of arriving at good answers, but it will take them longer and there is always a danger of their memory overloading and then needing to reboot. These twin deficits of working memory and processing speed are responsible for many of the everyday experiences of individuals who are dyslexic, dyspraxic or have ADHD in that they influence and shape their lives in many significant ways.

Provided a neurocognitive profile is reasonably flat, it is legitimate to use the test scores to calculate what is known as a Full Scale IQ. However, when the profile is spiky it is irresponsible to do so, for the figure that is calculated masks the strengths of that individual as well as their weaknesses. For example, Rosanna's performance on the tests of verbal and visual reasoning places her within the 'high average' banding, while her working memory score puts her in the 'low average' band. If this advice is disregarded and a Full Scale IQ calculated when spikiness is present, the resulting overall figure would put Rosanna within the average band. This is misleading and very unhelpful. Her scores on verbal and visual reasoning are the best indicators of her intellectual abilities, and her scores for working memory and processing speed are better seen as being mental scaffolding for these intellectual abilities. When this mental scaffolding is not as strong as it should be, it results in frustration and under-performance unless appropriate supportive adjustments are put in place.

Working memory

Working memory refers to the capacity to remember verbal information for a short period of time. It is like a voice in your mind. It used to be called short-term memory but the term 'working memory' is now preferred as it better captures how the voice in your head works. It is an active rather than a passive process. But it is of limited capacity. For example, if I were to ask how many letters there are in the word *forest*, this would require thinking about how the word is spelt and then counting the letters. Provided their spelling is not bad, this is a task many people could undertake without undue difficulty. Now imagine being asked how many letters there are in the word *hippopotamus*. This is a much more challenging task even if you can spell *hippopotamus* without difficulty, for the voice in your head has to work within a limited capacity.

One component of working memory is known as the phonological loop. This is rather like a loop of tape that mentally repeats what you have just said or thought. For example, when counting how many letters there are in *hippopotamus*, you might start by thinking *hippo* has five letters. This thought is placed onto your phonological loop to keep it on repeat in the background while you go on to focus on the next part of the word, *pot*. This has three letters, which need to be added to the previous five letters, the number you have been repeating to yourself. You then need to move to the last letters while keeping the number eight fresh in memory. This exercise is a relatively simple multi-tasking one and yet it is quite challenging. It requires much more working memory capacity than when counting how many letters there are in the word *forest*. Some individuals can bypass this memory limitation by being able to mentally 'see' the word. However, most people do not have this option.

For many individuals with a specific learning difference there is a mismatch between verbal reasoning skills and working memory, in that their working memory capacity is proportionally much smaller than it should be. This results in a number of difficulties, including multi-tasking. For example, when making notes in a lecture or taking minutes in a meeting, you have to be able to remember what has just been said, decide whether it is important enough to write down, and write it down at the same time. On top of this, if you are dyslexic and have to think how a particular word is spelt, making notes becomes even more difficult. This is captured in Illustration 1.1 below in which Hannah depicts her feeling of being overwhelmed with information in a lecture. Irrespective of whether it is dyslexia, dyspraxia or ADHD that is present, many people report having considerable difficulties with taking notes in lectures or meetings. Consequently, they either make notes without being able to follow what is being said or stop making notes and listen.

A limited working memory capacity also impacts on the writing of essays and reports. Many of the individuals I see recall being told by teachers that their essays contain excellent ideas, but the organisation is weak. Writing an essay is a form of story-telling, with a distinct beginning, middle and end. It requires many skills. You have to remember what you have read or viewed; decide what to include and what to leave out; remember who said what, and when, and where; you have to organise your ideas. All of these aspects require conscious thought and an ability to hold them in working memory. You also have to think about punctuation, spelling and your choice of words when writing, which also require working memory. While writing, you have to remember what you have already written (so as to avoid repetition) and, at the same time, think about what you still need to include. It is not surprising that when there is a shortage of working memory capacity the flow of

Illustration 1.1

written ideas becomes like a stream of consciousness, as the high level of multi-tasking required becomes impossible. Thoughts are written down as they occur and extensive editing is then required. Editing also requires working memory as a judgement has to be made about which ideas are more important than others, and this can only be done by considering those ideas simultaneously. It is therefore not surprising that the handwriting speed of individuals with specific learning differences is slower than that of their peers. The more working memory capacity there is, the greater the ability to multitask.

Reading is another process that requires multi-tasking. You need to be able to read words and understand their meaning; take note of punctuation and grammar; remember what you have just read; you need to decide what is important. If you stop to think about an unfamiliar word, this switch of focus can easily take up so much working memory capacity that the details of what you have just read are lost. Even if reading skills are good, it is very easy for working memory capacity to become overloaded when reading for information. This feeling of being overwhelmed by information when reading is a very typical one (see Illustration 1.2). Reading for academic purposes is very different from reading for pleasure. When engaged in recreational reading you can flow with the story, but when reading an academic text every word is important.

Working memory is a complex phenomenon. Although the capacity appears to be fixed this will vary with stress, when it seems to shrink, and automaticity, which results in an enhancement. Many activities, such as learning to

Illustration 1.2

drive, play a musical instrument, learn a language or new sport, initially place heavy demands on working memory capacity when you first start to learn them. For example, if you want to learn to play the guitar you need to learn to play chords. Initially, you have to make an effort to remember the notes for each string. You also have to think about the position of your fingers for each new chord. If you set out to master eight basic chords this will place an initial heavy strain on working memory and you will need to keep referring to a diagram of the positioning of each finger for each chord. This calls into play another aspect of working memory, and that is visual memory. The mental process responsible for capturing and displaying this kind of information is known as the visuospatial sketch pad.

Once again, this sketch pad is of limited capacity and holds visual and spatial information for just a short time. However, this also has to be converted into verbal information as you think about where to place each finger for each chord: 'for that string I need to be two frets up, the next finger only one fret up'. Over time, the process will become automatic and this will free up working memory capacity so you can then move on to the next stage. The smaller the working memory capacity, the longer it will take to achieve automaticity. This is why learning the times tables, a new language or rules of a game can seem to take forever. Rhodes *et al.* (2016), in their research demonstrating a clear link between doing well on a science test and working memory, refer to the 'well established link between working memory and a range of areas of academic learning' such as reading, languages and maths (p262). For example, when the times tables have been mastered and become automatic, carrying out mental arithmetic tasks becomes easier as less working memory space is taken up with thinking about the tables, thus leaving more available for working on the specific problem.

There are other features associated with working memory that are crucial to understanding how it works. These include how information enters into working memory and how this information is retained once it has entered consciousness. Because working memory capacity is limited, we are consciously aware of only a small fraction of the information being processed by the brain at any one time, even if that capacity is good. Imagine you are walking along and talking with your friends as you make your way to a local café. While you are engaged in conversation, your brain is also having to process information about your spatial position (so you don't bump into your friends, other people or objects such as street furniture), street noises (e.g. traffic, sounds from shops, other people), mentally keep an eye on the route you are taking and be alert to signs of danger or interest.

Most of this processing of information takes place unconsciously, but it is being prioritised. This prioritisation is aided by a cognitive process known as the executive function. It is as if the executive function is constantly scanning all the streams of information being processed by your brain and deciding which one should be brought to your attention. For example, you and your friends might be so engaged in conversation you walk past the café. The executive function will then switch your focus of attention from what is being said to an awareness that you have just walked past the café. Although executive function controls access to working memory, prioritisation is more difficult when working memory capacity is very limited.

When there is a big gap between a person's verbal reasoning ability and their working memory capacity, it is as if the executive function's ability to prioritise becomes overwhelmed due to too many thoughts trying to gain entry to a very limited space. When the pressure becomes too great, the ability to control the flow of thoughts and their order of entry into consciousness becomes less effective. This loss of control also results in thoughts being swept out of consciousness as new ones flood in. Illustration 1.3 is Hannah's depiction of her thoughts going off in random directions. If ADHD is present this is experienced to an even greater degree and is aptly captured in the nickname Jake's friends gave to him, 'Out of the Blue'.

Illustration 1.3

The executive function is also linked with the default mode network for it plays a role in controlling which state of awareness we are in. One state is that of being consciously engaged in a task, for example, when cooking and deciding the order to do things in. The alternative state is more of a form of mentation, such as recalling past memories of events you have experienced, thinking about the future and daydreaming. This alternate state of thinking, a mind-wandering state, requires a separate brain network, the default mode network, to the one involved in dealing with the reality of tasks in the here and now.

By playing a role in switching between these two states this can be thought of as another form of executive control prioritisation. Most people will be familiar with the experience of their mind drifting while making a journey they have made many times in the past. However, most individuals usually have a reasonable amount of control over conscious thought and can stop themselves going into involuntary, daydreaming default mode. But with ADHD in particular, the executive function slips into default mode much more easily. This may be because an ADHD individual often reports that it feels like a thousand thoughts are being experienced at once. This is a heavy cognitive load. Crittenden *et al.* (2015) have proposed that the default network mode is called into action 'whenever large changes of cognitive context are required'. This is what the ADHD brain is doing as it rapidly flits from one thought to another. Consequently, this may require the ADHD brain to spend more time in default mode and is therefore more likely to enter a daydreaming state.

Once information has entered working memory you usually need to hold it in your consciousness for a few minutes. For example, if you are introduced to a new person and told their name, it is embarrassing to realise you have forgotten it only seconds later. You need what I call *stickiness*. A dyslexic medical student used this analogy when asking why he could not be like his girlfriend, 'She reads something once and it just sticks in her memory. I read something three or four times and it doesn't stick'. It is as if a thought or idea that enters consciousness needs, as it were, a little bit of Velcro to give it stickiness. When there is a restricted working memory capacity, it is as if thoughts are more often slippery than sticky and come and go quickly. For example, you might think, 'I need to collect my shoes from my bedroom', only to get there and find yourself asking, 'What did I come here for?'. This slipperiness is particularly noticeable when ADHD is present. Individuals with ADHD, when not in a hyper-focused mode, will often describe themselves as having a racing brain. This refers to their experiencing a large number of thoughts rushing through their conscious mind, with the consequence that life can become chaotic with slipperiness rather than stickiness prevailing. This leads to issues with time management, 'Even a simple thing like making a cup of tea takes longer than it should'. It also leads to appointments being missed. Another consequence is the tendency to misplace items. When someone arrives to see me with a big bag, it is usually a sign they are prone to misplacing items. By putting everything they think they may need into one big bag they know that, somewhere inside, is the item they will need next. (See

Illustration 1.4). Rosanna's comment, 'My life is in my bag,' captured well her attempt to be more organised. When someone describes themselves as being disorganised, this is a heavy hint a working memory weakness is present.

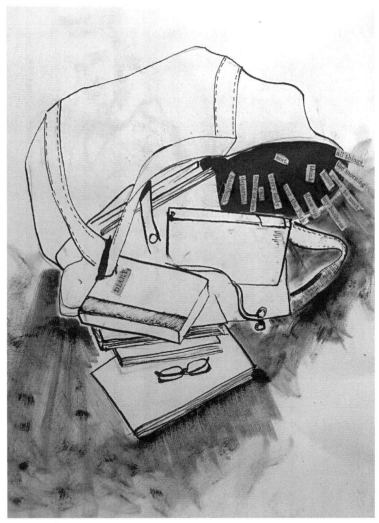

Illustration 1.4

Working memory is just one of a number of different types of memory. Some people have an excellent visual memory and are visual rather than verbal learners. Such individuals will report being very good at remembering people's faces but not their names. One fashion student I met developed his very own strategy for disguising this by calling everyone 'Dearie', an option not open to many. Visual memory can be powerful. For example, when there is a working memory weakness people find it difficult to remember directions. If there is a sequence of four or five instructions to remember, such as 'Carry on along this road for 200 metres, then turn left at the Red Lion. After two blocks take the next right into Scotland Road and then turn left at the next junction and you will be there', working memory will be overwhelmed by the time the person giving directions has finished. It is embarrassing to ask for them to be repeated. However, for those with a good visual memory, having made the journey just once they have no problems remembering the route the next time as they replay their mental sequence of images of landmarks.

One common technique to help with the planning of essays and reports is mind-mapping. This is a visual technique that makes use of line diagrams, colours and symbols to cluster ideas and create a structure for the points to be made. This enables the stream of thoughts to be captured on paper (or, even better, on a computer screen) and then organised. This overcomes the 'slipperiness' issue because ideas and thoughts have been written down before they disappear. I remember the occasion when I was demonstrating this technique to a dyslexic student. As I did so he became very interested and explained why, as he pointed to the screen and said 'That's the way I think'.

Processing speed

A slow processing speed is as much a part of the pattern of commonality between dyslexia, dyspraxia and ADHD as a weak working memory. Processing speed primarily refers to speed of processing information. It is measured in different ways, including how quickly you can scan a row of mixed symbols, such as green triangles and red squares, and cross out rogue symbols (such as green squares), and also the speed of remembering associations between numbers and symbols while drawing the symbols. The first of these tasks is a very visual one, placing strong demands on visuospatial memory, while the second involves a combination of verbal and visual memory, allied with fine hand–eye coordination.

Most everyday activities require a high degree of integration across a number of specialised areas in the brain. When a slow processing speed is present, it is as if the neuronal networks that link one part of the brain to another are running slowly. This is rather like a slow broadband speed taking more time than it should to download and upload information, and the connection sometimes failing because it is taking too long for different regions of the brain to talk to each other. This becomes quite noticeable when an individual's profile is very spiky and shows a sizeable deficit for processing speed. On tests with no time constraints, such as those assessing knowledge of vocabulary, the pause between asking a question and a reply is often quite noticeable. But as long as the individual is not put under pressure, they often produce answers of a very high standard. However, when put in a situation where a fast and careful answer is required, for example when giving a presentation or in a class discussion, they then tend to feel quite vulnerable and avoid such situations if they can. A very slow processing speed also results in under-performance in timed tests and exams.

When there is a slow processing speed, it is as if the individual is able to think faster than they can scan lines of text or put their ideas in writing. This can result in them losing their place when reading, or missing out parts of a word or a phrase when writing. The impact of a very slow processing speed can be seen very clearly in Grace's test score profile (Figure 1.4).

Her spiky profile also reveals one of the variations in neurocognitive functioning that is often observed. Whereas

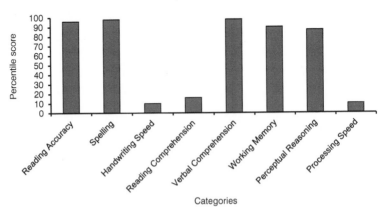

Figure 1.4 Grace's profile – the impact of a very slow processing speed

Grace scored highly on measures of verbal and visual reasoning and on working memory, her processing speed test figure places her within the bottom 10 per cent of the population for her age group. In comparison, her working memory score is in the top 10 per cent. In spite of having excellent reading and spelling skills, her test scores for reading comprehension and speed of handwriting are well below expectation. These tests are time limited. Grace is a drama student and in comparison with other actors she is slow at learning lines, in spite of a having reasonably good working memory capacity. She also described herself as being a slow reader and at school she was slow at copying from the blackboard. My diagnosis for Grace was ADHD.

Cheryl's profile (Figure 1.5) is different from Grace's, as she has a fast processing speed but a significant working memory weakness. My diagnosis was dyslexia. Cheryl's reading and spelling scores are weak, so it is not surprising she struggled when tested on her speed of reading for comprehension. However, in spite of her fast processing speed, her handwriting speed is also below expectation. Cheryl had represented her county at both the 100 and 200 metres so, in physical terms, she is fast. However, her handwriting speed is slow. This is a reflection of her dyslexia allied with her working memory weakness rather than a lack of fast motor coordination. Using the analogy of the brain as a computer, when the processing chip is very fast but the RAM very limited, the speed at which information can be downloaded into memory is much faster than the capacity to handle it, so the system is likely to crash quite frequently.

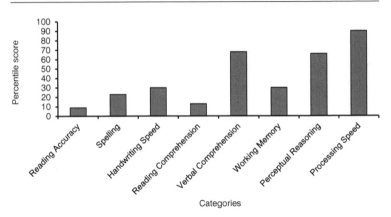

Figure 1.5 Cheryl's profile – a variation on the typical dyslexia
profile

A slow processing speed can influence the kind of
computer games that are preferred. 'Shoot and kill' or
racing games require fast reaction times. If you have a slow
processing speed you are more likely not to do very well
and games of strategy become the preferred choice. A slow
processing can also impact on sporting performance if success
involves having a fast reaction time. For example, someone
with good spatial awareness but a slow processing speed is
more likely to play in defence than as a forward in team
games such as football or hockey. However, this observation
is only a generalisation. Commitment and enthusiasm
are two of the key attributes to developing a high level of
sporting skills. For example Niall, who is dyslexic and has
ADHD and a slow processing speed, pointed out that while
his motor coordination for most sports is 'not great,' he has
'a real passion' for football (both Gaelic football and soccer).
Consequently, as a result of many hours of practice each week
over a number of years, by the time of his teens he 'was the
best' and was selected to play for his county.

Many studies report the cognitive double deficit of working memory and processing speed as being a common feature of dyslexia, dyspraxia and ADHD, but we are a long way from understanding the reason for this commonality. Although these are fundamental neurocognitive processes, they appear to be quite fragile. I occasionally see individuals who have suffered brain injury as the result of an accident. Typically in these cases both working memory and processing speed are disrupted and it can sometimes take years for full recovery to take place.

While this double deficit is typically observed in about 70 to 80 per cent of people who are dyslexic, dyspraxic or have ADHD, there is no causal linkage, since one deficit can be present without the other, as is clear from the profiles for Grace and Cheryl. However, in order to understand the lived experiences of individuals who are dyslexic, dyspraxic or have ADHD, it is necessary to move beyond the core defining diagnostic behaviours of these specific learning difficulties and adopt a holistic perspective.

References

Brown, T.E., Reichel, P.C., & Quinlan, D.M. (2011) Extended time improves reading comprehension test scores for adolescents with ADHD. *Open Journal of Psychiatry*, 1: 79–87 doi:10.4236/jsemat.2011.13014

Crittenden, B.M., Mitchell, D.J., & Duncan, J. (2015) Recruitment of the default mode network during a demanding act of executive control. *eLife* 2015 (4): e06481 April 13. doi: 10.7554/eLife.06481. Last accessed August 6, 2016.

Rhodes, S.M., Booth, J.N., Palmer, L.E., Blyth, R.A., Delibegovic, M., & Wheate, N.J. (2016) Executive functions predict conceptual learning of science. *British Journal of Developmental Psychology*, 34 (2): 261–275.

Chapter 2

What is dyslexia?

If you were to ask the question 'What is dyslexia?' you would anticipate a reply along the lines of it being about reading difficulties. However, the answer is not so simple, which is why – for some – dyslexia is still a controversial diagnosis (e.g. Elliott & Grigorenko, 2014). Unlike dyspraxia, where a UK consensus has been reached, and ADHD, where there is a European consensus statement (Kooij *et al.*, 2010), there is no such general agreement as to the key criteria for defining dyslexia. For my part, I have argued for some years that it is more helpful to think of dyslexia as taking different forms, as it being far more than just a difficulty with reading and for the need to avoid automatically assuming that all reading difficulties are due to dyslexia.

Whenever I carry out a diagnostic assessment I ask for an estimation of both the total number of books the individual has read for pleasure from cover to cover and also how many others they have started to read but never finished. I also enquire about their style of reading, i.e. their speed of reading and how well they remember what they have just read. Of the responses to these questions given by four individuals (see below), just two of the four were diagnosed as being dyslexic, one was dyspraxic and the other had a diagnosis of ADHD. Can you identify which two are dyslexic?

1 It is only occasionally that Elizabeth engages in reading for pleasure, usually when she is on holiday. She found it difficult to estimate how many books she has read for pleasure from cover to cover, but eventually suggested about two a year. She has also started but never finished 'too many' others. Elizabeth described her speed of reading as being 'very, very slow' and attributed this to difficulties with remembering what she has just read. If she stops to think about the pronunciation of a word she forgets the beginning of the sentence she has started to read.

2 Philip did not read for pleasure as a child and this is still very much the case. 'Reading is an arduous thing.' He described how, when reading a text for the first time, 'it is just a mixture of words' and he has to reread to understand the text. Philip estimated he has read no more than ten books (excluding textbooks) for pleasure from cover to cover and has started perhaps twenty to thirty others that he has never finished.

3 It is only since she was about sixteen that Sophie has taken to reading for pleasure. She estimated she has read about sixty books (excluding textbooks) from cover to cover and has started another ten to fifteen

that she has never finished. Sophie mentioned she has difficulty remembering what she has just read.

4　Prior to starting school Lucy's parents spent time trying to teach her to read and write but 'I didn't quite seem to get it.' Soon after starting school Lucy's sudden switch to being able to read was so rapid she recalled her father saying, 'It's like a miracle. She can read.' When reading a textbook for information she has to read 'more than once'. Lucy mentioned that in the sixth form she would often still be reading a passage when others had finished and begun discussing it. She found it very difficult to estimate how many books (excluding textbooks) she has read for pleasure from cover to cover but eventually suggested it is probably in the hundreds.

It's not surprising if you are finding it difficult to decide who is dyslexic and who isn't. I have encountered too many misdiagnoses to be surprised by mistakes. When ADHD is present, remaining focused while reading is frequently a serious challenge. Just one word can result in that person's mind going off on a journey of its own, with the consequence they forget what they have just read and never reach the end of the page. When Philip refers to reading being an 'arduous process' he is referring to just how hard it is for him to stay focused. For example, on reading the sentence, 'The couple had just returned from Brighton' he might immediately start thinking, 'It's a long time since I visited Brighton. I wonder if Jean is still there. She had a marvellous sense of humour.' Philip has ADHD.

In life in general his mind 'goes its own way', with the consequence that he frequently abandons a book after just a few pages. Many individuals with ADHD report starting but not finishing many more books than they have read from cover to cover. This is the case for Philip.

As it is possible for someone to have both ADHD and dyslexia, it is necessary to determine whether Philip's reading difficulties are not just due to attentional issues. The closest the UK currently comes to having a consensus on the key features of dyslexia is the Rose Report (2009). It defines dyslexia as being 'a learning difficulty that primarily affects the skills involved in accurate and fluent word reading and spelling' and continues by stating that while the 'Characteristic features of dyslexia are difficulties in phonological awareness, verbal memory and verbal processing speed', the core defining features are lack of word reading accuracy allied with lack of word reading fluency.

When Philip was asked to read aloud an extract taken from a broadsheet newspaper without having to remember what he had just read, his speed of reading aloud was a fast 212 words a minute. This is 3.5 words per second, which is slightly faster than the undergraduate norm I have established of 3.3 words per second. Philip's speed was only achieved when he used a yellow overlay. Without the overlay his speed dropped to 3 words per second, since visual stress was present (see Chapter 7).

When Philip was tested on his ability to read individual words, his accuracy was good (top 14 per cent for his age group). He opted to use a yellow overlay when undertaking this reading test. On placing the overlay over the list he

was surprised by the positive change in his perception of
the words, 'they've stopped vibrating'. Philip's word reading
accuracy score was slightly higher than his overall score for
his verbal reasoning skills. Since he is able to read with both
accuracy and fluency, he is not dyslexic. However, when
tested on his ability to read for comprehension, Philip's score
was very low (see Figure 2.1 below). This is a reflection of
his difficulties with staying focused while reading, allied with
problems with remembering what he has just read. Although
there is a significant reading difficulty, Philip is not dyslexic.
In general, when ADHD is present a slowness with reading
for comprehension is to be anticipated (Brown *et al.*, 2011)
and this justifies additional time in exams.

Although Sophie has read about six times more books
than Philip, and she is younger than him, she is dyslexic.
While reading for pleasure is something a number of
dyslexics wish they could engage in, there are some who
do enjoy recreational reading in spite of having difficulties

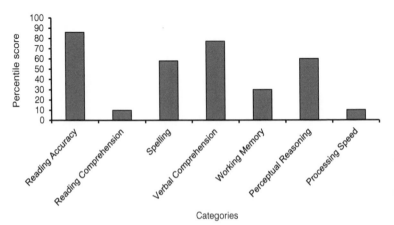

Figure 2.1 Philip's profile

with word recognition and lack of fluency. Sophie's reading speed of 2.8 words per second is about 15 per cent below expectation. While her test score profile (Figure 2.2) reveals her reading accuracy and reading comprehension skills are well matched, both are well below her level of verbal reasoning skills. Her verbal reasoning figure places her within the top 5 per cent of the UK population for her age group. In sharp contrast, her word reading accuracy score is in the bottom 34 per cent. This means that Sophie's ability to use and understand vocabulary when talking or listening is well above her ability to read with accuracy, even familiar words. This disparity is crucial to arriving at a diagnosis of dyslexia.

However, such an imbalance, by itself, cannot be taken as definitive confirmation of dyslexia. It has to be placed within the wider context of developmental history and everyday life. In Sophie's case her reading difficulties were recognised by her primary school teachers and she was

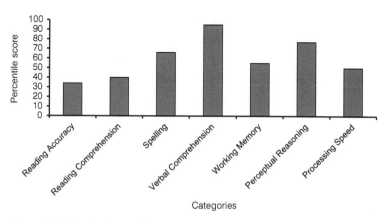

Figure 2.2 Sophie's profile

provided with additional reading tuition. When she was 15 she was formally diagnosed as being dyslexic. As there is a long-standing history of reading difficulties, and these have persisted in spite of additional teaching, the case for arriving at a diagnosis of dyslexia is strengthened. Sophie's academic performance at school also reveals typical dyslexic-type features, such as her preferring more practical subjects (e.g. the sciences, design technology) to essay-based ones (e.g. history, religious studies), and her very noticeable difficulties with learning a foreign language. When learning to play the clarinet she had particular problems with learning to read music.

While it cannot be considered to be a defining feature of dyslexia, Sophie's spiky neurocognitive profile reveals a weak working memory and a slow processing speed, a profile that is frequently recorded when dyslexia is present. As pointed out in Chapter 1, this spikiness means it is misleading to use IQ as a comparison point for reading scores. This spikiness is also central to appreciating why being dyslexic is much more than just a literacy weakness. For example, a working memory deficit impacts on everyday life, such as forgetting to pass on phone messages, needing to make shopping lists and difficulties with calculating change when shopping. It also influences everyday experiences, such as having to work harder than peers when writing, reading and revising.

Lucy's neurocognitive profile is very similar (see Figure 2.3), in that both a working memory weakness and slow speed of processing are present. However, her Perceptual Reasoning score reveals a visual reasoning weakness

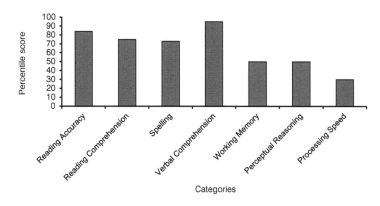

Figure 2.3 Lucy's profile

present as well, which is a sign that dyspraxia may be present. However, Lucy's scores for word reading accuracy and reading comprehension are close to her level of verbal reasoning. In spite of an early history of initially being slow at learning to read, Lucy is not dyslexic. She is dyspraxic. In many cases, when there is a weak working memory and a slow speed of processing, the learning of a new skill will be a slow process to begin with. However, this can be followed by rapid progress once automaticity is achieved, which was the case for Lucy.

Elizabeth's history was typical of many people seeking assessment. In spite of attending a private primary school with small class sizes, it was not until she was approaching the end of high school that it was finally recognised she had reading and spelling difficulties, primarily because her marks for exams were much lower than for essays. Her speed of reading (2.4 words per second) is about a third below expectation and her word reading accuracy score places her at the population midpoint. If Elizabeth were of average intellectual ability this would not be an issue. However, her verbal reasoning is within the top 2 per cent of the population and, at university, she would be expected to be able to read academic texts with fluency. In employment, she would be expected to be able to read and understand technical reports.

Elizabeth's school reports often described her as being quiet in class, hard-working and as having difficulty drawing upon previous knowledge and applying it. It was as if Elizabeth had made herself invisible in class in order to avoid drawing attention to the problems she was experiencing. Through working exceptionally hard she had masked just how long it took her to read, write and absorb information. However, in exams there was no hiding and Elizabeth's slowness at reading and writing were exposed. Although her reading and spelling skills lie within the average range, she is under-performing in comparison with others of her intellectual level. She is dyslexic.

If Elizabeth were to undertake a diagnostic assessment in the United States it is highly likely she would be given a diagnosis of 'Specific Learning Disorder with Impairment in Reading' rather than a diagnosis of dyslexia. In the US, assessment criteria and outcomes are frequently carried out in accordance with the standards set by the Diagnostic and Statistical Manual of Mental Disorder (DSM). While it is not obvious why dyslexia should be considered as part of the remit of the body of clinicians who decide the nomenclature and assessment criteria for a wide range of mental health conditions, it is nevertheless a publication that American educational psychologists adhere to.

The fifth and most recent edition, known as DSM-5, was published in 2013. Because of continuing concerns about the variety of definitions of dyslexia, it is recommended that the diagnosis of 'impairment in reading' be used in place of 'dyslexia'. While the caveat 'Dyslexia is an alternative term used to refer to a pattern of learning difficulties characterized by problems with accurate or fluent word recognition, poor decoding, and poor spelling abilities' is added, the use of 'dyslexia' as a diagnostic outcome is discouraged. However, it is still a legitimate diagnosis to reach. Because the alternative diagnosis of 'impairment in reading' is a broader one, Philip could potentially have been given this diagnosis in addition to his diagnosis of ADHD. However, since ADHD is known to result in a slowness when reading for comprehension (i.e. due to difficulties with staying focused and with remembering), such an additional diagnosis is unnecessary.

A key feature of both the Rose Report and DSM-5 is the emphasis they place on the identification of the specific nature of the reading difficulties a given person is experiencing, so that teaching can be designed to remedy them. This philosophy is endorsed by Elliott and Grigorenko (2014) who argue for 'the need for assessment for intervention rather than assessment for diagnosis' (p580). The Rose Report goes much further than DSM-5 in that it provides a framework across the early years for identifying reading difficulties, with the acknowledgement that these are wider than those subsumed by a diagnosis of dyslexia.

The implementation of mandatory phonics teaching in English primary schools represents a serious attempt to improve reading skills for all. In part it also reflects a current belief held by many that a phonological weakness – a difficulty with learning the correspondence between sounds and sequences of letters – is the core cognitive deficit that results in dyslexia. For example, having reviewed four decades of research on dyslexia, Vellutino *et al.* (2004) conclude,

> the research strongly suggests that reading difficulties in most children are caused by deficits in phonological coding. Such deficits are believed to account for the reliable and robust differences observed between poor and normal readers on measures of phonologically based skills such as phonological awareness, alphabetic mapping, phonological decoding, verbal memory, and name encoding and retrieval (p30).

This conclusion is, in my opinion, open to criticism. For example, the statement 'reading difficulties in most children are caused by deficits in phonological processing' does not apply to individuals with ADHD, who frequently have problems with reading comprehension, or to individuals who are dyspraxic, for whom forgetfulness and difficulties with visual tracking can be significant issues. As there are different forms of difficulties with reading, I would have preferred the phrasing '*dyslexic-type reading difficulties* …'. Second, as individuals with ADHD or dyspraxia typically have much better phonological processing skills in spite of a working memory deficit, it is highly unlikely a phonological processing deficit gives rise to a verbal memory deficit *only* when dyslexia is present.

There is also the question of whether dyslexia takes just one form – a phonological one. Although the word 'dyslexia' was first used by the German ophthalmologist Rudolf Berlin in 1887, early accounts of dyslexia, e.g. Morgan's classic paper about Percy (1896), preferred the diagnosis of 'congenital word blindness'. That is, a difficulty with reading words accurately in spite of a high level of verbal ability was attributed to some form of visual deficit. Over a hundred years later the predominant view is now one of dyslexia as a linguistic deficit. However, it is not inevitable that a phonological deficit is recorded when word reading skills are poor. In 2014 Julia Carroll reported that a recent study of poor readers she and her colleagues carried out had recorded 'deficits in phonological awareness, short-term memory, visual search and rapid naming each occurred in 30–40 per cent of the sample' (p24). In a separate paper Carroll *et al.* (2014) raise the question of whether phonological processing is a unitary factor, for their survey found poor readers from families at risk of dyslexia did worse on tests of Nonword Repetition and spelling, while the comparison group of poor readers did worse on Nonword Learning. They conclude dyslexia probably results from a combination of two or more deficits rather than a single deficit.

There is a long history of describing individuals with word reading difficulties as falling into one of three categories. For example, in 1945 Schonell refers to

children who are visually weak readers (e.g. confusing
b and d and transposing letters, e.g. *brunt* for *burnt*),
auditorily weak readers (e.g. confusing *th* and *f*) and
readers who have a combination of both. In 1973 Boder
proposed the same categorisation, introducing the terms
'dyseidetic' and 'dysphonic' for visually weak and auditorily
weak readers respectively. (NB: An alternative name for
dyseidetic dyslexia is 'surface dyslexia'.) Those with the
combined difficulties did not have a specific categorisation.
More recently Dehaene (2009) provides evidence that,
while the majority of dyslexics have a core impairment
in the processing of speech sounds, 'another, smaller,
number of children probably suffer from a primarily visual
impairment' (p294).

There is other evidence phonological processing is not
the sole answer. A number of studies report that when
dyslexic individuals are asked to rapidly identify and name
a range of familiar symbols such as letters and numbers,
or colours, they are slower than non-dyslexics. This test is
known as the Rapid Automatized Naming Test (RAN).
While it has been argued that rapid naming is another
aspect of phonological processing in that it requires
an ability to gain quick access to verbal information
held in long-term memory, other researchers question
this. For example, Araújo and her colleagues (2011),
having reviewed the evidence, conclude, 'At least one
component of the rapid naming performance ... appears
to reflect an underlying deficit that is independent of a
phonological deficit' (p208). This conclusion should not
come as a surprise, for Sophie's test profile (Figure 2.2)

is a characteristic dyslexic one, revealing both a working memory weakness and a slow processing speed. But since a slow processing speed is also a characteristic feature of both dyspraxia and ADHD, it is difficult to argue it is a good measure of phonological processing. In my opinion, a major failing of virtually all dyslexia research is that no comparison has been carried out with individuals, such as dyspraxics or people with ADHD, who have a very similar neurocognitive profile of a weak working memory and a slow processing speed, but who also have good word reading accuracy skills.

When a visual reading weakness is present, but not a phonological one, Boder (1973) has provided evidence that an individual with dyseidetic dyslexia will experience significantly more difficulties with reading irregular rather than regularly spelt words. Regular words follow phonetic spelling rules, so that if your ability to match sounds to letters is reasonable you will be able to arrive at the correct pronunciation of a word even if it is one you have seldom encountered, such as the botanical name *Papaver* for poppy.

Irregular words, such as yacht, sword and paradigm do not have a direct relation between letters and sounds and so cannot be 'sounded out'. Whereas some languages, such as Spanish, Italian and Latin, are regular languages (sometimes referred to as being transparent or phonetic languages), English is notorious for being highly irregular. This can result in social embarrassment. When Aisha asked another student whether the café they were sitting in had We Fee, she blushed with shame when told it was pronounced Wi Fi. English also contains many homophones, that is words with the same pronunciation but very different meanings and spellings. For example, if you ask the question, 'What source would you like with your pasta?' your error would not be noticed. However, if you were to write source instead of sauce your mistake would be instantly recognised. Phonetics has its limitations. Visual memory is also important, particularly when reading and spelling in English.

Gavin said he has never read a book from cover to cover in his life. In his first year at secondary school he was placed in what he called 'the dunces' class' but the following year he was moved up to the top class for English. Even though he disliked being asked to read aloud in English classes, because his reading skills were poor, his teacher frequently asked him to do so. It was not until he was an undergraduate on a TV Production course that Gavin was formally recognised as being dyslexic. His word accuracy reading score placed him in the bottom 23 per cent of the population. However, in sharp contrast, his spelling score put him in the top 27 per cent. His ability to read regular words was over three times better than for irregular ones. When spelling, he is good at mapping letters onto sounds, which may be why his spelling ability is much better than his word reading. Gavin's test performance revealed much stronger phonic than visual skills, which is indicative of dyseidetic dyslexia. This is why I prefer the term 'dyslexias' rather than 'dyslexia'. By differentiating between the different forms of poor word reading ability, teaching support can be more precisely targeted.

It is important to note that, while it is helpful to know what form of dyslexia is present, the names given to these forms are only descriptive ones. They are not in themselves explanations, and this is captured most vividly in Stein's (2015) proposal that the 'phonological theory' be scrapped 'because it is not really a theory: it merely repeats in different words that dyslexics have difficulties with reading. What we need is an understanding of the basic visual and auditory sensory processing impairments that cause these difficulties' (p14).

There is a large body of complex and highly technical research focused on attempts to identify the underlying biological and cognitive processes that result in word reading difficulties. As yet there is no general consensus. However, one promising approach is the visual attention (VA) span deficit hypothesis (e.g. Bosse *et al.*, 2007). When reading, VA has to be paid to each word and, when sounding a word out, VA has to become even more specific and be paid to each letter in the word. These forms of micro-analysis are very rapid, taking place in microseconds. There is evidence that, irrespective of which form of dyslexia is present, this very basic process is less efficient than in individuals with competent word reading skills, leading Bosse *et al.* to claim that 'the present study provides evidence for the VA span disorder as a potentially second core deficit in developmental dyslexia' (p36).

The disconnection between Gavin's poor word reading skills and his much better spelling is why I focus on the core defining features of poor word reading accuracy skills and lack of reading fluency when considering whether dyslexia is present. While there is often a close match between reading and spelling skills, it is not an inevitable one. For example, Philip's reading skills are noticeably better than his spelling ability. I often record such a disparity when ADHD is present and suspect it may stem in part from a low tolerance for routine tasks. Some people rely on muscle memory when spelling. This memory is built up through writing out a word many times until it becomes automatic. This is precisely the kind of task an ADHD individual will avoid.

In contrast, Elizabeth's spelling is better than her word reading accuracy. Her school reports all refer to her as being hard-working. In addition, she said that when working out the spelling of a word she tries to picture it. On being taken through a short series of names of capital cities she said she could 'see' each word. The letters lacked colour. In contrast, Philip is unable to visualise a word when arriving at a spelling and instead relies on 'sounding it out'.

Even when a language is phonetically regular, dyslexic-type difficulties are still observed. For example, Shanar lived in Iraq until she was thirty, when she moved to work in the UK. Her parents spoke both Kurdish and Arabic and she said she can speak both fluently. Shanar said these languages share a common alphabet but the spoken languages are quite different. They are both regular languages but with different phonetic systems. In spite of their regularity, Shanar had problems with learning to read in both Kurdish and Arabic 'especially in Years 2 and 3' and she still has a memory of a primary school teacher telling her off because she was reading slowly, 'Hurry up. Why are you struggling?". In spite of being able to read in Arabic, Shanar has never read for pleasure and has difficulty remembering what she has read. Even though she is good at maths she had problems learning the times tables. She was slow at copying from the blackboard at school. When she became a teacher of computing studies in Iraq, it took her a long time to learn the names of her pupils.

Shanar's test profile is a typical dyslexic one and her poor working memory is the key to understanding why she struggled with activities such as learning the times tables and pupils' names. It was not until Shanar had lived in the UK for some time and enrolled as a Computing Engineering undergraduate that she was formally diagnosed as being dyslexic. Like many individuals with a specific learning difference, the subjects she opted to study were influenced by the need to avoid her weaknesses and play to her strengths. At school, her marks for maths and physics (in the 1970s) were always much higher than for Arabic (in the 1950s). It is not surprising that she opted for the sciences pathway in high school and followed this by enrolling on an electronic engineering diploma programme. In her late thirties, in England, Shanar then enrolled on a degree course in computing.

When English is a second or third language, additional caution is required in arriving at a diagnosis of dyslexia and the personal history becomes particularly important. As knowledge of English vocabulary may also be weak, this makes it even more difficult to differentiate between dyslexia and specific language impairment, for a specific language impairment gives rise to dyslexic-type features.

'Dyslexia and specific language impairment … are now often regarded as different manifestations of the same underlying problem, differing only in severity or developmental stage' (Bishop & Snowling, 2004, p858) and they impact on both reading comprehension and reading fluency. In Shanar's case there was no evidence of language development difficulties in her early years, so an alternative diagnosis of specific language impairment could be discounted.

In Chantelle's case, English is her native language so differentiating between dyslexia and specific language impairment was easier. She was a music student who had only just passed the Year 1 and Year 2 written technical exams in spite of working hard preparing for them. One of her tutors suspected she might be dyslexic and advised her to seek a diagnostic assessment. When I met Chantelle she described herself as having always felt somehow different from others and this had affected her self-confidence. She said she has a stammer and it became apparent that she has a slight lisp as well. Chantelle said her major difficulty is 'lack of consistency, even in speech' and gave as examples her long-standing mispronunciation of *pomegranate*, *Valerie* and *duvet* (which she still pronounces *juvet*). She is prone to 'confusing words that sound the same and look the same' such as *specific* and *Pacific*. Chantelle recalled being told by teachers at school she had 'missed the point again' in exams.

Chantelle's word reading skills were average, as was her knowledge of vocabulary. However, when tested on her understanding of the sematic links between words (e.g. how are *young* and *elderly* conceptually similar?) her level of understanding was very high, in the top 1 per cent of the population. She also performed very highly on tests of visual reasoning. It was clear there was a long standing specific language difficulty, a diagnosis that was more appropriate than one of dyslexia.

Although the emphasis so far in this chapter has been on the core defining features of dyslexia and the need to avoid assuming that all reading difficulties should be attributed to dyslexia, many dyslexics report problems with writing, both in terms of organising their ideas when writing and with forgetting what they were about to write if they stop to think about how to spell a word. Both of these difficulties result in a slowness when writing. However, when dyslexic students have undertaken a creative writing composition exercise, there is no question about their ability to produce high quality work.

Esther Freud is a highly regarded novelist who has written at least eight novels. She is also dyslexic. Natasha Solomon is another successful novelist. She was unable to read until she was eight, and was thirteen before she was diagnosed as being dyslexic. To date she has published two novels (one of which is being made into a film). Her view on dyslexia is that she prefers to 'think I just see the world slightly differently from other people. I see odd connections between things, and I like to think that my brain's natural chaos enhances my creativity.' (2010, p28). There are many examples of individuals with dyslexia who have struggled with the literacy demands of education but then gone on to be very successful in their chosen careers. Margaret Rooke's book, *Creative, Successful, Dyslexic*, is a good starting point for exploring this further.

References

Araújo, S., Faísca, L., Petersson, K.M., & Reis, A. (2011) What does rapid naming tell us about dyslexia? *Avances en Psicología Latinoamericana* Bogotá (Colombia), 29 (2):199–213.

Bishop D.V., & Snowling, M.J. (2004) Developmental dyslexia and specific language impairment: same or different? *Psychological Bulletin*, 130 (6): 858–86.

Boder, E. (1973) Developmental dyslexia: a diagnostic approach based on three atypical reading-spelling patterns. *Developmental Medicine & Child Neurology*, 15 (5): 663–687.

Bosse, M-L., Tainturier, M-J., & Valdois, S. (2007) Developmental dyslexia: The visual attention span deficit hypothesis. *Cognition*, 104 (2):198–230.

Brown, T.B., Reichel, P.C., & Quinlan, D. M. (2011) Extended time improves reading comprehension test scores for adolescents with ADHD. *Open Journal of Psychiatry*, 1: 79–87. doi:10.4236/jsemat.2011.13014. Available at: http://www.scirp.org/journal/PaperInformation.aspx?PaperID=7817. Last accessed August 11, 2016.

Carroll, J.M. (2014) Phonological processing: Is that all there is? *Dyslexia Contact*, 33 (1): 22–24.

Carroll, J.M., Mundy, I.R., & Cunningham, A.J. (2014) The roles of family history of dyslexia, language, speech production and phonological processing in predicting literacy progress. *Developmental Science*, 17 (5): 727–742. Available at: www.researchgate.net/publication/260443198_The_roles_of_family_history_of_dyslexia_language_speech_production_and_phonological_processing_in_predicting_literacy_progress

Dehaene, S. (2009) *Reading in the Brain. The Science and Evolution of a Human Invention*. Viking, Penguin Books, London.

DSM-5 (2013) *Diagnostic and Statistical Manual of Mental Disorders: DSM-5*. American Psychiatric Association, Washington, DC.

Elliott, J.G., & Grigorenko, E.L. (2014) *The Dyslexia Debate*. Cambridge University Press, Cambridge.

Kooij, S.J.J., *et al.* (2010) European consensus statement on diagnosis and treatment of adult ADHD: The European Network Adult ADHD. *BMC Psychiatry*, 10: 67. Available at: http://bmcpsychiatry.biomedcentral.com/ articles/10.1186/1471-244X-10-67

Morgan, W.P. (1896) A case of congenital word blindness. *British Medical Journal*, 7 November, 2: 1378.

Rooke, M. (2015) *Creative, Successful, Dyslexic*. Jessica Kingsley Publishing, London.

Rose, J. (2009) *Identifying and Teaching Children and Young People with Dyslexia and Literacy Difficulties*. An independent report from Sir Jim Rose to the Secretary of State for Children, Schools and Families, June 2009. Available at: www. education.gov.uk/publications/eOrderingDownload/00659-2009DOM-EN.pdf. Last accessed August 16, 2016.

Schonell, F.J. (1945) *Backwardness in the Basic Subjects*, 2nd edition. Oliver & Boyd, Edinburgh & London.

Solomon, N. (2010) I thought that there were two separate languages: one sounds and one squiggles. *Evening Standard*. July 14, 27–28.

Stein, J. (2015) The dyslexia debate. *Dyslexia Contact*, 34 (3): 12–14.

Vellutino, F.R., Fletcher, J.M., Snowling, M.J., & Scanlon, D.M. (2004) Specific reading disability (dyslexia): what have we learned in the past four decades? *Journal of Child Psychology and Psychiatry*, 45 (1): 2–40.

Chapter 3

What is dyspraxia?

Kaylee first became aware she was somehow different from others when she was four. Her mother had enrolled her in ballet classes, but after about a dozen lessons she realised she was clumsy compared with the other girls in her group. She also found it very hard to remember sequences of steps, and her slowness at learning was commented on negatively by others. Her sense of shame and embarrassment resulted in her begging her mother to stop taking her to ballet lessons, which she did. At nursery school Kaylee's teachers became concerned by her difficulties with forming shapes and letters. Her problems with mastering handwriting continued into primary school and she was the last in her class to progress from using a pencil to a pen. Kaylee described her schoolwork as always looking scruffy, no matter how hard she tried to be neat.

In primary school Kaylee came to dread Physical Education (PE). She described herself as having poor hand-eye coordination as she was not good at throwing or catching. She also has a poor sense of balance and would stumble and fall over when running. She could never master skipping. Being the last to be chosen for a team helped reinforce Kaylee's sense of being different. Because she found it so hard to learn to tie shoe laces, her mother eventually only bought her shoes with Velcro fastenings. Kaylee also struggled with plaiting her hair. As a teenager she gave up using makeup for, whenever she applied nail polish or eye-liner, it would be smudgy. When travelling on an escalator she always stands and holds the handrail. Even crossing a road causes a brief moment of anxiety as she has trouble judging speed and distance.

Kaylee has always loved reading and, by immersing herself in books, created a world she felt secure in and enjoyed. At secondary school she discovered she was good at learning foreign languages. She was best at written translations but speaking and listening came less easily. Maths was quite a challenge, as were art classes. Kaylee loved the history of art but described her drawing skills as being stuck at the stick man level. Because she was very slow at copying from the blackboard her school permitted her to use a laptop in class as her typing speed was much faster than her handwriting. Kaylee said that when writing by hand it is as if her brain is thinking much faster than she can commit her ideas to paper. However, by using a laptop there is a better match between her speed of thought and speed of writing. When Kaylee's school realised she never managed to finish exams in time, with the result that her exam marks were much lower than for coursework, she was eventually permitted to use a laptop in exams as well. Kaylee found this very helpful because 'cutting and pasting' enabled her to better organise her thoughts when writing.

Kaylee did well enough in her high school exams to be offered a place at several universities. Because she enjoyed reading, and loved English literature at school, she began a degree in English. When Kaylee asked whether she could use a laptop in her university exams she was told this was not possible unless she had a formal diagnosis confirming she has a specific learning difference. When I met Kaylee I asked whether she was clumsy or well-coordinated as a child. She replied she was clumsy, 'always breaking things, always falling over', and is still clumsy nowadays. Because she bumps into things so frequently she always has several bruises, which she calls her 'mystery bruises'. She often drops things and has broken five or six mobile phones to date. When eating out Kaylee avoids choosing pasta dishes, and eating a meal on a plane 'is a nightmare, I have to do everything so slowly'. If cooking for herself, she finds it difficult to use a can opener.

The core defining feature of dyspraxia is a continuing history of clumsiness/poor motor skills that impact negatively on everyday life (including educational activities). I diagnosed Kaylee as being dyspraxic and she was then permitted additional time and the use of a computer in her exams. At her assessment session Kaylee also described herself as being 'disorganised' and she was subsequently provided with study skills support to help improve her note-taking, the organisation of class handouts and academic papers and essay-writing skills. Several years later Kaylee graduated with First-class Honours and obtained a scholarship to enrol on a PhD programme. Equally as important as her academic success was the positive change in her self-esteem. Having the diagnosis enabled Kaylee to attribute her clumsiness to being dyspraxic rather than to being stupid. Following the assessment her mother wrote to say that Kaylee 'found the assessment most enlightening and it proved to be a huge relief, as your comments helped her to come to terms with some of the difficulties she has been experiencing'.

Kaylee's experience of not being diagnosed as dyspraxic until she was 19 is not unusual. There is still a lack of awareness about this specific learning difference, which has not been helped by the lack of agreement about what name to give to this specific learning difficulty or by confusing definitions (Drew, 2005). Until the 1980s dyslexia was viewed primarily as a medical condition, a perspective echoed in terms such as 'clumsy child syndrome' and 'minimal brain dysfunction'. In recent years there has been a major step forward in the UK for, following two meetings of Movement Matters (November 2011 and January 2012) a UK consensus was reached on the definition of dyspraxia. These meetings also agreed that the alternative diagnostic term of 'Developmental Co-ordination Disorder (DCD)' could be used interchangeably with 'dyspraxia'. The consensus agreement states:

> Developmental Co-ordination Disorder (DCD), also known as Dyspraxia in the UK, is a common disorder affecting fine or gross motor co-ordination in children and adults. This lifelong condition is formally recognised by international organisations including the World Health Organisation.

DCD is distinct from other motor disorders such as cerebral palsy and stroke and occurs across the range of intellectual abilities. Individuals may vary in how their difficulties present; these may change over time depending on environmental demands and life experience.

An individual's co-ordination difficulties may affect participation and functioning of everyday life skills in education, work and employment. Children may present with difficulties with self-care, writing, typing, riding a bike and play as well as other educational and recreational activities. In adulthood many of these difficulties will continue, as well as learning new skills at home, in education and work, such as driving a car and DIY. There may be a range of co-occurring difficulties which can also have serious negative impacts on daily life. These include social and emotional difficulties as well as problems with time management, planning and personal organisation and these may also affect an adult's education or employment experiences.

In addition to reaching an agreement on a definition, it was also agreed that, as there is no single test for dyspraxia, specialist assessors such as psychologists can arrive at a diagnosis of dyspraxia for adults by taking a detailed developmental history. This is a vital agreement, for while it is necessary to record longstanding and still present examples of problems relating to clumsiness and/or motor coordination in order to arrive at a diagnosis of dyspraxia, specialist assessors can also provide important information on educational and neurocognitive strengths and weaknesses. In addition, specialist assessors are also able to diagnose other specific learning differences, particularly ADHD and dyslexia.

When dyspraxia is present, reading and spelling skills are usually in line with verbal reasoning ability, but handwriting speed is typically slow and the handwriting itself is often untidy. In addition, a working memory weakness and quite a slow processing speed are frequently recorded. Part of Kaylee's assessment involved her undertaking the ten core tests that are part of the Wechsler Adult Intelligence Scale 4th Edition test battery (WAIS-IV). Her test scores (Figure 3.1) illustrate this typical spiky profile. Frequently the overall figure for visual reasoning skills (Perceptual Reasoning) is lower than for verbal reasoning ability (Verbal Comprehension). However, the figure for Perceptual Reasoning needs to be read with caution for, when dyspraxia is present, it can mask a major discrepancy between the three test scores used in its calculation.

Two of these test scores (Block Design and Visual Puzzles) are measures of the ability to mentally manipulate visual shapes, while the other test – Matrix Reasoning – is more like doing written algebra, a form of visual logic. The first two are measures of spatial ability while Matrix Reasoning is a measure of nonverbal reasoning. Kaylee's scores reveal a typical dyspraxic disparity in that she achieved a much higher score on the nonverbal reasoning test than on the tests of spatial ability, and by looking at her profile you can see just how big this disparity can be. This is not a

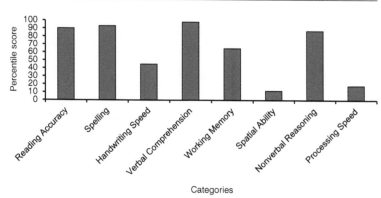

Categories

Figure 3.1 Kaylee's test profile

surprise, for a meta-analysis of research papers by Wilson and McKenzie (1998) revealed a weakness in complex visuospatial information processing is the predominant information-processing deficit associated with dyspraxia.

A spatial ability weakness will have an impact on particular skills. Kaylee was asked about her sense of direction and she replied she is always getting lost. Consequently, when she has to study or work at a new location it takes her much longer than others to learn her way around. The only way she can remember which is left and which is right is by forming an 'L' shape with her thumb and fingers. When using the London Underground, it takes her some time to work out whether she needs to get on a train going west or east. Kaylee recalled being poor at geometry but good at algebra. As a child she could never do jigsaw puzzles. When packing for holiday, her case is usually untidy as she finds it difficult to mentally picture how she can make the best use of the available space.

Craig was more fortunate than Kaylee in that he was first diagnosed as being dyspraxic when he was in secondary school. However, the only concession his school granted was additional time in exams. As a university student he required an up-to-date assessment. When asked whether he was well coordinated or clumsy as a child, Craig replied he was 'not well coordinated ... I still can't catch, I was never any good at football'. Like Kaylee, he has bruises from bumping into objects. He is also very prone to breaking and spilling things. On the one occasion he worked in a bar he was so slow at collecting glasses because of taking care not to drop any that he was not invited back. Craig hated having to take part in sports at school, particularly football and rugby. He recalled being hit by a football 'so many times'. (NB: A fear of being hit in the face by a ball is often mentioned by individuals who are dyspraxic.)

Craig's educational and neurocognitive profile is very similar to Kaylee's in that his reading and spelling skills are very good but his handwriting speed is slow. He has very good verbal reasoning skills but there are weaknesses in visual reasoning and working memory, and particularly in processing speed. Craig said he is very familiar with the comment that although his essays contain excellent ideas, the organisation is poor. He also finds it hard to take details in quickly when reading for information. At school he preferred maths to humanities subjects because he did not have to write essays for maths and could work things out from first principles. Craig had not realised this was a reflection of his neurocognitive profile, for the combination of a weak working memory and a slow speed of processing slow down the speed at which information can be taken in and ideas structured. Dyspraxia is far more than just a motor-coordination weakness. It impacts on the ability to undertake a wide variety of everyday tasks that require specific forms of mental thought.

When individuals with a specific learning difference are asked whether they are well-coordinated or clumsy, they sometimes reply they are disorganised. While disorganisation is not a defining characteristic of dyspraxia, it can arise because a limited working memory capacity frequently results in forgetfulness, such as not remembering appointments and misplacing items. Even when dyspraxic individuals develop strategies that reduce the need to undertake various physical activities, such as using public transport instead of driving, limiting the use of makeup, being careful what they choose to eat in restaurants or buying a protective case for their mobile phone, the neurocognitive profile still has an impact on everyday life.

When I met Chris he was in his mid-sixties. Although it was over fifty years previously, he still recalled his embarrassment when his woodwork teacher at secondary school 'had to give me someone else's bookstand to take home because I couldn't even finish mine'. His practical skills are still poor and he pointed out that he still finds undertaking DIY tasks in his house 'very stressful'. Consequently, he frequently puts off doing things. He 'hated' team sports at school 'and once tried to hide behind the goal post'. By the time he left school at sixteen his level of self-esteem was low and he had few friends.

At school Chris experienced the same problems as Kaylee and Craig in terms of being slow at writing and taking in information. However, as he attended school in the 1950s and early 1960s he was viewed by his teachers as just being slow and no support was provided. He under-performed in some exams and this became very much the theme of his adult life. He was slow at working on routine, paper-based tasks. Low self-esteem was also an issue and Chris failed to complete a teacher training programme due to lacking self-confidence when having to face a classroom of children. When working as a civil servant, promotion was 'a distant dream'. Even when working as a volunteer teaching English as a second language he found himself unable to keep up with the required record keeping. In spite of Chris's verbal reasoning skills placing him within the top 1 per cent of the population, his weak working memory and quite slow processing speed have had a strong negative impact throughout his life. It was not until Chris was in his sixties that his first formal diagnosis of dyspraxia resulted in him being provided with appropriate study skills support and exam accommodations for the part-time degree course he had recently commenced.

It is not always straightforward to decide whether dyspraxia is present. For example, on being asked whether she was well-coordinated or clumsy as a child, Ellen replied that she was 'well-coordinated'. However, when the different forms that clumsiness can take were explored with Ellen she said she does bump into things, 'I am constantly covered in bruises'. She also spills things, knocks things over and drops items. In addition to losing about six mobile phones in the past six years she has damaged 'either four or five' through dropping them. However, Ellen 'loved sports' at school and said she was particularly good at gymnastics. She enjoyed a wide range of sports and was, at various times, a member of her school lacrosse, hockey, netball, swimming and athletics teams. She recalled being 'always first or second' at swimming and athletics. Since leaving school Ellen has spent some years working as a chef and she described herself as being very fast at slicing.

Ellen's developmental history reveals some classic signs of dyspraxia as well as major contra-indications. Her WAIS profile is not a classic dyspraxic one as her highest test scores were for speed of processing. Her overall score for these tests places her within the top 5 per cent of the population. In addition, her verbal and visual reasoning skills were similarly high. However, there was a major working memory weakness. I diagnosed Ellen as having ADHD, not dyspraxia. Her fine and gross motor skills are excellent, as is her sense of spatial awareness. When Ellen's clumsiness was discussed with her she attributed her bumping into things and dropping items to being 'impulsive, rushing about, and not paying attention'.

There is good evidence that when dyspraxia is present there is a high probability it will be accompanied by another specific learning difference (e.g. Peters & Henderson, 2008). The co-occurrence of dyspraxia with ADHD is well known, and in the 1980s Scandinavian researchers (e.g. see Gillberg, 2003) reported that about fifty per cent of children with dyspraxia also had ADHD. Because this incidence of co-occurrence was so high a new diagnosis of DAMP (deficits of attention, motor control and perception) was proposed. Some years later this option was dropped by Scandinavian clinicians for the more standard one of Developmental Coordination Disorder with ADHD.

About 40 per cent of the individuals I see who are dyspraxic also have ADHD and about 15 per cent are dyslexic. Because of the high degree of co-occurrence, as the case of Ellen illustrates, considerable care has to be taken to avoid arriving at a wrong diagnosis. Whereas Ellen's personal history reveals very good motor coordination, Alisha's shows wide-ranging motor coordination difficulties. Alisha's mother has always called her clumsy and Alisha said this is still the case, and gave as an example falling over the previous week and ripping her new abaya. She said she knocks 'everything over' and is always spilling liquids, 'juice, water, tea'. Alisha mentioned she was fired on her first day of working as a waitress because she was so clumsy. She rarely uses make-up because she finds it so time-consuming to put on. Alisha disliked PE and sports because she was 'bad at it'. She began learning to play the guitar when she was at primary school but gave up after a couple of years as she was unable to coordinate her hands, 'How can you do two things at the same time?'. Alisha's mother has encouraged her to learn dressmaking and embroidery skills but without much success as she has trouble threading a needle and sewing neatly. Alisha said that when using a compass to draw circles 'the ends never meet'. Alisha's diagnosis was one of dyspraxia with ADHD (of the Inattentive form), for her history also revealed long-standing issues with concentration, distractibility, procrastination and rapid changes of mood. Unlike Ellen, Alisha's clumsiness and problems with motor coordination cannot be adequately accounted for through lapses of attention and impulsivity.

In comparison with dyslexia and ADHD, dyspraxia is very much under-researched. For example, whereas it is well established that both dyslexia and ADHD are highly heritable, ADHD even more so than dyslexia, little is known about the underlying causes of dyspraxia. In my experience, about 50 per cent of dyspraxics report a history of birthing difficulties. This was true for both Chris and Alisha. Chris's birth was two weeks late and followed an emergency Caesarean section. While Alisha was born at full-term, labour was difficult and delivery was forceps-assisted. She was a big baby at about 9lbs. If there is a genetic basis for dyspraxia, it is highly likely to be a less dominant causal feature than is the case for dyslexia and ADHD, and birthing factors may be much more important.

Due to this lack of research, the proportion of females to males with dyspraxia is uncertain. For example, Kadesjö and Gillberg (1999) report a male/female ratio varying from 4:1 to 7:1 for boys compared with girls. In contrast, Cairney et al. (2009) report a finding of 41 per cent boys and 59 per cent girls in their cohort of primary school children. My experience is that I see roughly equal numbers of males and females who are dyspraxic. It may be that dyspraxia is recognised earlier in boys than girls, since boys value more highly active participation in physical activities, particularly sports, than girls (Cairney et al., 2009), with the consequence that clumsiness and poor motor coordination become more noticeable. This, in turn, may also result in an earlier onset of anxiety and lowering of self-esteem. Obvious clumsiness is also likely to mark a child out as being different from others, and many individuals who are dyspraxic report being subjected to bullying. It is often not until dyspraxics are at university that they feel more socially comfortable, in that intellectual ability then contributes significantly to self-esteem. However, even then real potential will only be obvious to others when appropriate support and assessment accommodations are in place.

The relative lack of research on dyspraxia is matched by the lack of public understanding and awareness of dyspraxia. Whereas it is very easy to name famous individuals who are dyslexic or have ADHD, it is only relatively recently that a few well known people have announced they are dyspraxic. One of the first to do this was Daniel Radcliffe who has spoken of his difficulties with tying shoelaces and his poor handwriting. More recently, in 2014 when answering a question from a mother about her dyspraxic daughter, he said 'It has never held me back and some of the smartest people I know are people who have learning disabilities. The fact that some things are more of a struggle will only make you more determined, harder working and more imaginative in the solutions you find to problems.'

Florence Welch, of Florence + the Machine, echoes this need for being imaginative. Speaking at a dyspraxia event in Dublin in 2008 she said she was diagnosed as being dyspraxic in her childhood and that it had 'not caused too much trouble so far'. She attributed this to 'the fact that I work in a creative industry (which) probably helps. In fact I think in some ways it has helped. We dyspraxics think in a different way.' Regrettably, not everyone who is dyspraxic is diagnosed at an early age. The adage 'knowledge is power' is certainly applicable to individuals who have a specific learning difference.

References

Cairney, J., Hay, J.A., Veldhuizen, S., Missiuna, C., & Faught, B.E. (2009) Developmental coordination disorder, sex, and activity deficit over time: a longitudinal analysis of participation trajectories in children with and without coordination difficulties. *Development Medicine & Child Neurology*, 52: 67–72.

Drew, S. (2005) *Developmental Co-ordination Disorder in Adults*. Whurr Publishers Ltd, London.

Gillberg, C. (2003) Deficits in attention, motor control, and perception: a brief review. *Archives of Diseases in Childhood*, 88: 904–910.

Kadesjö, B., & Gillberg, C. (1999) Developmental coordination disorder in Swedish 7-year-old children. *Journal of the American Academy of Child and Adolescent Psychiatry*, 38 (7): 820–8.

Peters, J.M., & Henderson, S.E. (2008) Understanding developmental coordination disorder (DCD) and its impact on families: the contribution of single case studies. In Sugden, D.A., Kirby, A., & Dunford, C. (Eds) *Special Edition of the International Journal of Disability, Development and Education*, 55: 97–113.

Wilson, P.H., & McKenzie, B.E. (1998) Information processing deficits associated with developmental coordination disorder: A meta-analysis of research findings. *Journal of Child Psychology and Psychiatry*, 39 (6) 829–840.

Website references

Daniel Radcliffe (2014) 21 random questions with Daniel Radcliffe. Available at: http://blogs.wsj.com/speakeasy/2014/10/28/21-random-questions-with-daniel-radcliffe/. Last accessed June 6, 2016.

Florence Welch (2008) Dyspraxia has good points – Florence. Available at: www.irishtimes.com/news/dyspraxia-has-good-points-florence-1.532002. Last accessed June 6, 2016.

Chapter 4

What is ADHD?

When Hazel was asked why she leaves revision and the writing of course assignments until the last minute she replied 'I work best under pressure … I am the queen of procrastination'. It is not just academic work that Hazel puts off until the last minute – procrastination is also a feature of her everyday life. She gave as an example not buying her sister a birthday present even though she had decided several weeks in advance what she would buy. Even when she gets up in plenty of time to leave for university it is always a last minute rush to gather everything together: 'I don't know where the time goes'. Hazel's habit of putting off doing things until the last minute is a classic ADHD behaviour, one I refer to as the 'good intentions syndrome'. In spite of wanting and needing to do something on time, it gets left until the last minute, or is not done at all. These constant failures then become a source of stress, anxiety and frustration.

When Hazel was at school her teachers recognised she was intelligent but were puzzled by her erratic performance. In class tests her marks would often be poor but, somehow, she would perform well in exams. When homework was handed in for marking (and not all homework was done) it was usually late but frequently of a very good standard. At open evenings Hazel's parents were frequently told that she had potential, if only she could apply herself to her studies. They were also told that Hazel was easily distracted and not well organised, as she would often forget to bring with her the books and notes she required for the day's lessons.

Through last minute cramming Hazel achieved sufficiently good A-level grades to enable her to attend her first choice university. Throughout her last couple of years at high school she had been undecided about which subject to study at university but had eventually opted for anthropology as the idea of learning about different cultures, with the possibility of travel, appealed to her. Hazel has always found it easy to make friends but maintaining relationships is more difficult. She greatly enjoyed the first couple of months of being at university but then began to struggle with the need to be self-motivated and self-organised.

Because Hazel leaves the writing of essays until the last minute – 'too much thinking, not enough doing', she spends many late nights struggling to meet deadlines. At school she had been taught how to answer essay questions using a template approach, but at university she has to decide for herself how to structure essays. Because she finds it difficult to organise her thoughts – 'there are too many … they are all racing around' – her first draft is often 'chaotic and disorganised'. Partly because she is 'a bit of a perfectionist', panic then sets in as she struggles to achieve the academic standard she knows she is potentially capable of.

By the time Hazel was halfway through her second year her self-esteem was low and her anxiety level high. She has had marks deducted due to late submission of work, and because she started revision at the last minute, her exam marks were below expectation. It is very difficult for her to work in a library due to her hyper-sensitivity to noise and movement, 'the sound of someone typing on a keyboard drives me to distraction'. Time management is also a problem. Hazel is often late for morning lectures and for meetings with friends. There are also occasions when she forgets to take her ID card to university.

Hazel first realised her study difficulties might be due to factors other than her being lazy or stupid when discussing them with a fellow student who said Hazel sounded very much like his sister who has a diagnosis of ADHD. This initially came as a surprise to Hazel, for her idea of ADHD was a stereotypical one of boys behaving badly. However, following a diagnosis that confirmed she does have ADHD, of the form known as Inattentive ADHD, she described how this diagnosis provided her with a new lens to view herself through, one that made much more sense of her life: 'Such self-awareness is going to help me achieve what I aspire to do in the future, although it will take a great deal of self-discipline, organisation and research. I feel ready for this now.'

It has been recognised for some time that ADHD takes different forms. For some individuals, such as Hazel, attentional difficulties are the main issue, whereas for others attentional difficulties are combined with hyperactivity and impulsiveness. For a few, hyperactivity and impulsiveness are the dominant behaviours. About 50 per cent of the individuals I see who have ADHD have the form known as Inattentive ADHD, and about 50 per cent of these are female. There is evidence (Brown *et al.*, 2009) that the Inattentive form of ADHD is the most difficult to spot, especially when an individual is intelligent, has supportive parents, and has attended a school with good teachers. These features provide what Brown *et al.* call 'scaffolding', which serves to keep a propensity towards procrastination and disorganisation in check. It is only when the young person enters higher education and/ or leaves the family home and has to take much greater responsibility for being self-motivated and self-disciplined, that the cluster of inattentive behaviours that are a key feature of Inattentive ADHD come to the fore. Hazel's comment, 'I now have too much freedom [at university]' captures this change and challenge.

Hazel's initial surprise at learning she has ADHD was a typical reaction, at least in the UK. In spite of ADHD having a written history that stretches back to 1798, in the UK it was not until 2008 that NICE (the National Institute for Clinical Excellence) formally advised that not only is ADHD a valid condition, but it is also one that can apply to both adults and children. Consequently, there is a very high number of children and adults in the UK whose ADHD is undiagnosed. (NB: The current convention is to use the term ADHD for all forms of ADHD/ADD. The type of ADHD is then given in brackets – e.g. ADHD [Inattentive presentation].)

There are a number of misconceptions about what ADHD is. For example, it is not true that people with ADHD are completely unable to concentrate. Although Hazel reported often finding it very difficult to stay focused while reading and writing, there are occasions in lectures or when holding a conversation, when the opposite is the case. For example, if the lecturer is charismatic and talking about a topic that really interests her, and the lecture is interactive, she can then become intensely engaged. These periods of being hyper-focused are, to her regret, rare. It is as if her ability to maintain focus has an on/off switch but no dimmer dial, so her mental ability to hold on to a conscious thought for a few minutes is in either 'slippery' or 'sticky' mode.

Some people with ADHD find that engaging in risky activities causes them to be hyper-focused. For example, Conrad Anker, a high altitude mountaineer who has ADHD, talks about how doing something risky puts him 'in the moment'. It is as if, by engaging in a potentially dangerous activity, the brain of an individual with ADHD self-medicates and he/she becomes intensely focused, having switched into 'sticky' mode. Louis Smith, the UK's greatest Olympian gymnast prior to the Rio Olympic Games, 2016, has ADHD. He has described how, when practising on the pommel horse, gymnasts are well aware that 'every moment could be their last', for one mistake can result in serious injury and the end of their career (2014). Consequently, Louis has to be hyper-focused at all times when performing. Other risky activities include being a stand-up comedian

Illustration 4.1

and Rory Bremner, a famous UK comedian, has spoken of ADHD as being his 'best friend, but worst enemy' (2014).

These three individuals have ADHD of the Combined form i.e. inattention coupled with hyperactivity and impulsivity. This is also the case for Neil. When I met Neil he was studying to be a paramedic. He described himself as being unable to stay focused for more than a couple of minutes and his school reports were full of references to his attentional difficulties and disruptive behaviour. Neil's mother described him, when young, as being 'an energetic little boy who loved being active, playing rugby, climbing trees, playing rough & tumble games'. He has always enjoyed taking part in sports, preferring more extreme activities such as mountain biking and white water kayaking. One year an exasperated teacher wrote 'Neil does not have concentration problems when kayaking!'. Nor does he have concentration problems when attending a medical emergency. However, as soon as he sits down to read an academic paper or write an essay he quickly becomes fidgety and restless, and loses focus very quickly. His life history is typical of someone with the combined form of ADHD – inattention coupled with hyperactivity and impulsivity.

Another myth is that ADHD is predominantly limited to males. Like Neil, Anna also has the combined form of ADHD. Anna's mother described her as being a real problem child at nursery as she was 'always active, always on the go'. At primary school, several of the teachers took to sitting her at a table by herself at the front of the class. At secondary school Anna was a member of almost all the sports teams in spite of never excelling at any sport. Anna described herself as being both physically and mentally restless, 'When I am on the go I am a whirlwind.' In her rush to do something she is prone to breaking things or bumping into objects.

Anna is intellectually very able. However, this factor, combined with her impulsivity and lack of patience, resulted in her getting into arguments with teachers at high school and she was frequently described as being disruptive. At university she is finding it almost impossible to sit through a lecture or spend time in a library. Her failure to engage effectively in activities that other students seem to find easy has become a source of serious concern to her, and her growing sense of being both a failure and stupid is increasingly resulting in periods of high anxiety and black moods.

Anna said she has always experienced rapid mood swings, from happiness to frustration, from calm to anxiety. She is also hyper-sensitive to noise, movement and the emotional mood of others, 'I pick up on the emotional moods of others very quickly'. This is also the case for music. Anna loves dancing and described herself as responding 'very emotionally to melody and lyrics'. There is a growing recognition that emotional volatility is a key ADHD characteristic and both Anna and Neil reported experiencing rapid changes of mood. It is as if the difficulties they experience with trying to control the mental rush of their thoughts are mirrored by their struggle to maintain emotional control.

Anna is also a synaesthete and the way she mentally experiences the world is very complex. Not only do letters have colours and feelings, but so do numbers. She experiences C as being yellow and happy, while G is orange and stout; 3 is yellow with a crunchy texture; 4 is dark green with a velvet softness; 8 is blue and slippery. Words frequently trigger complex mental responses for Anna. For example *medieval* instantly conjured up mental pictures of a banqueting hall, candles and tapestries, and at the same time she 'heard' Greensleeves being played on a lute; *Tuesday* triggered a flash of colour, 'pond green with a touch of teal'. There are occasions when Anna's simultaneous mental mixture of verbal, visual, emotional and textural sensations is so rich that it results in sensory overload.

The incidence of synaesthesia is much higher when ADHD is present, and there is evidence that synaesthetes have a greater range of colour discrimination than non-synaesthetes (see Chapter 6). Synaesthesia is an aspect of hyper-sensitivity – the ability to notice more subtle forms of stimuli than others – and being distracted by them. For example, one music student told me that just hearing the soft sound of a hand being run over the arm of a chair distracted her. Another student reported finding the curls and swirls in a carpet or wallpaper distracting: 'they are so organic'. Occasionally this form of hyper-sensitivity can result in what appears to be obsessive compulsive behaviour, such as needing to have all their CDs or books precisely lined up in terms of height and/or colour.

Hyper-sensitivity can take many forms and occurs across all the senses. For example, some people are hyper-sensitive to the texture of some foods or materials (such as wool being scratchy). In my experience noise, movement, light and emotional mood are the most commonly reported ones. Hyper-sensitivity can, as it were, add an even greater loading to an already over-active mind. On occasions it results in sensory overload and the individual has to take time out, as one put it, 'to allow my brain to cool down'. Hyper-sensitivity is a characteristic that appears to be shared with individuals on the autistic spectrum, but in a less intense and less over-whelming form. However, in contrast with those on the autistic spectrum, individuals with ADHD positively seek out newness – new interests, new partners, new activities. Boredom is a constant threat.

Rhonda, a music student, caught this search for newness poignantly, 'My bedroom is a graveyard for instruments'. The same was true for Ellen. She described how she would take up a new instrument 'with a burst of enthusiasm' but after a time, when it became harder to improve, she would become frustrated, lose interest and take up a new instrument. She recalled learning to play eleven different instruments including the flute, fife, piccolo, violin, piano, guitar and ukulele. When I met her she was in her mid-thirties and was unable to recall the number of companies she had been employed by, mainly working as a chef or a waitress. This is quite typical of many adults with ADHD aged in their 40s and 50s, as they often report having spent short periods of time in a wide variety of jobs.

Another often overlooked feature of ADHD is that other specific learning differences are frequently also present. Probably the most frequently co-occurring specific learning difference is dyspraxia and there are reports from the 1980s that this co-occurrence might be as high as 50

Illustration 4.2

per cent. In my experience about 30 per cent of the ADHD individuals I see are also dyspraxic and about 20 per cent dyslexic. However, when ADHD is present a person may be clumsy without being dyspraxic, and reading problems may be present without that person being dyslexic. For example, Gareth described himself as being clumsy in that he often bumps into things and has broken a number of mobile phones through dropping them. However, his motor coordination and spatial awareness are very good as he has competed in mountain bike races for some years, and enjoys snowboarding and skiing. On discussing his clumsy behaviour with Gareth, it became clear they were due to his rushing to do things and his frequent lapses of attention. He is therefore accident prone because of his ADHD, not because he is dyspraxic. Gareth described himself as being a restless kind of person, both physically and mentally. He mentioned he has found that after taking part in a physically demanding activity his ability to stay focused improves for a while. For this reason Gareth has taken to spending time in a gym in the evening to enable him to settle down to university work.

Like many individuals with ADHD, Gareth has good word reading skills but in spite of this described himself as being a slow reader, 'I have to read it three times to take it in' (see Brown et al., 2011). Consequently, he often starts reading a book a book for pleasure but soon loses interest and puts it down, intending to go back to it. He often does not pick it up again and Gareth estimated he has started but not finished many more books than he has read from cover-to-cover. Because of his difficulties with taking in information when reading and with staying focused, even when he has started work in good time for an assignment he is easily distracted by other activities. He then finds himself rushing to meet a deadline and becomes angry and frustrated with himself for wasting time.

It is not surprising that many people with ADHD report having mental health problems. About 40 per cent of the ADHD individuals I see report having had one or more bouts of depression. In comparison, only 10 per cent of dyslexics and 20 per cent of dyspraxics report one or more bouts of depression. When ADHD co-occurs with dyspraxia, the frequency shoots up to about 60 per cent. However, it drops to about 20 per cent when ADHD co-occurs with dyslexia. While we cannot be sure why this decrease occurs, I strongly suspect that having a diagnosis of dyslexia is, in itself, sufficient to enable an individual to attribute all their difficulties to being dyslexic. In the UK dyslexia has been more widely recognised than ADHD, and is diagnosed at an earlier stage. When there is no obvious explanation for repeated failures other than being lazy and/or stupid, it is as if that individual is constantly beating themselves up. There is no doubt that, for many, being diagnosed as having ADHD is very liberating. Following her diagnosis of ADHD, Greta emailed the next day to tell me, 'I feel so relieved and I can learn not to be so harsh on myself now'.

When I first met Myra she was a struggling medical student. She was much better at practical than multiple-choice exams and got 'parts of words mixed up' when writing case notes. She also reported difficulties with maintaining focus in long briefings and being slow at reading. She was also what I describe as a 'time optimist' in that her time management was poor. In spite of allowing what should have been ample time to arrive for an appointment she was frequently a few minutes late. Myra is a visual learner – once she has created a visual image 'I've got it forever'. She is better at remembering faces than names, anatomy than genetics, and at remembering syndromes and diseases through meeting a patient with a condition rather than reading about it in a textbook. My assessment confirmed she was highly intelligent but was both dyslexic and had ADHD. About six years after her diagnosis Myra contacted me to let me know that following her diagnosis she had worked out a variety of strategies to help her succeed. After graduating she spent several years working in Australia and was now returning to a core surgical post in the UK.

Having ADHD need not be a barrier to success and there are times when hyperactivity and hyper-focusing result in outstanding performance. Yi Ling had enjoyed a successful career creating adverts for radio stations in south east Asia and had won a national award for the quality of her work. Writing copy for radio adverts was, in her words, a 24 hour/7 days a week career, and by her late thirties she wanted a less demanding working life, so she set up her own company. Her ADHD then became a hindrance rather than an advantage, in that she was now having to work to long deadlines and undertake many routine, boring tasks, such as stock taking, maintaining files, taking notes of meetings with clients and suppliers and sending out invoices. In order to prevent her company from failing she had to appoint a manager to handle the administrative side, thus allowing her to focus on her strengths in innovation and selling.

Li Ying's experience is very typical of many adults with ADHD and her strengths and weaknesses are echoed in Sonia's history. Sonia was once a university lecturer. When giving a lecture she was outstanding, but she struggled badly with the administrative requirements: 'My organisation is shocking – marking essays and exam papers, recording and reporting, all cause me to lose sleep. I do them, but the struggle is dreadful, and if I don't have a tight system to work within, they slide'. Because she did not know at the time she had ADHD, and because her struggle with fulfilling the administrative requirements were resulting in prolonged high levels of stress and anxiety, Sonia left the post she had coveted as a student.

David Bowie was world famous. It is not so well known that he had ADHD, and this appears to have been a key to his constant reinvention of himself. When being questioned in 1999 about this aspect of his creativity Bowie replied, 'I was a person who had a very short attention span and would move from one thing to another quite rapidly when I got bored with the other, and I became comfortable with that'. In the same interview he described himself as being drawn to his need 'to have a set of conflicts going on around me'. When relaxed he was not creative. However, when engaged intellectually and creatively, he was in his element.

This is also the case for Lucy. She has mild ADHD and is a music student training to be a singer. Following her assessment she emailed to explain, why, for her,

> I am glad that I have what I have ... it's made me the creative artist that I am today and this I know is to be looked on as a blessing, not a curse. I always knew that there was something a little different about me when in a rehearsal environment in comparison to others; I would always be incredibly excited, filled with an overwhelming feeling of contentment and enjoyment and would perpetually exert the parameters by putting 110 per cent into anything I was singing, dancing or acting. I suppose in a way, it helped me to stand out from the crowd. There is no place I would rather be than on a stage; performing to the best of my ability, using my vocal and acting skills to reach out to an audience and brighten someone's day/evening.

Background notes

In the UK, a medical diagnosis of ADHD is usually the province of a psychiatrist, as is the management of ADHD. Over the last decade it became increasingly obvious that there was a high number of students in higher education with undiagnosed ADHD. Furthermore, they were underperforming in academic terms (Pope *et al.*, 2007). The obtaining of a medical diagnosis of ADHD was, and still is, often a long and arduous process, but appropriate teaching and exam accommodations could not be provided by universities and colleges until a formal diagnosis of ADHD was available.

The UK may be unique in having a body (SASC – SpLD Assessment Studies Committee) that advises on diagnostic assessment standards for students with specific learning difficulties. In 2013 this committee convened a national consensus meeting to advise on the assessment of ADHD as a specific learning difficulty. In September 2013, SASC advised that 'practitioner psychologists and specialist teacher assessors *who have relevant training* can identify specific learning difficulties and patterns of behaviour that together would strongly *suggest* a student has ADHD; and in this situation they can make relevant recommendations for support at further and higher education institutions'.

This agreement was a major step forward in enabling students with undiagnosed ADHD to receive appropriate support in further and higher education. All the case studies cited in this chapter are based on individuals who were diagnosed by myself as having ADHD as a specific learning difficulty. It is important to note this is not a medical diagnosis. Advice was provided on steps they could take, if they wished, to obtain a medical opinion.

References

Brown, T.B., Reichel, P.C., & Quinlan, D. M. (2009) Executive function impairments in high IQ adults with ADHD. *Journal of Attention Disorders*, doi:10.1177/1087054708326113. Available at http://jad.sagepub.com/content/13/2/161

Brown, T.B., Reichel, P.C., & Quinlan, D. M. (2011) Extended time improves reading comprehension test scores for adolescents with ADHD. *Open Journal of Psychiatry*, 1: 79–87. doi:10.4236/jsemat.2011.13014 Available at http://www. scirp.org/journal/PaperInformation.aspx?PaperID=7817. Last accessed August 11, 2016.

Pope, D., Smith, C., Lever, R., Wakelin, D., Dudiak, H., & Dewart, H. (2007) Relationships between ADHD and dyslexia screening scores and academic performance in undergraduate psychology students: implications for teaching, learning and assessment. *Psychology Learning and Teaching*, 6: 114–120.

Smith, L. (2014) Guest Speaker. UKAAN 4th Congress: ADHD – Mind, Brain and Body. London, September 10–12.

Websites

David Bowie (1999) David Bowie speaks to Jeremy Paxman on BBC Newsnight *The BBC*. Available at: www.youtube.com/watch?v=FiK7s_0tGsg. Last accessed August 11, 2016.

Rory Bremner (2014) Living with ADHD is "hell". *The BBC*. Available at: www.bbc.co.uk/news/health-29794415. Last accessed June 24, 2016.

Chapter 5

What is dyscalculia?

When I was a psychology undergraduate we were taught statistics by a mathematician. Big mistake. We were not mathematicians and we were floundering. Several months before taking our final exams we were rescued by a lecturer who was a non-mathematician and understood our difficulties. When I became a psychology lecturer and was asked to teach statistics I took the decision to approach the subject in a very different way. Eventually I found one that was effective. In my first statistics session with students I asked them to complete a questionnaire which included rating themselves on a scale for maths anxiety. Over 70 per cent of the students reported having high levels of maths anxiety.

If someone has maths anxiety it is as if a mental barrier is put up every time they are asked to undertake a maths task or learn a mathematical procedure. Unless you can get past that barrier very little learning is going to take place. Putting their fears into the open led the students to feel more reassured. The next step was to teach them how to draw bar charts and look for patterns in sets of data they had generated about themselves. This was a gentle process and taken at a slow pace, but it resulted in students being able to look at a set of numbers and begin to appreciate the story they were telling. Once confidence is established and students can see why statistics is important, it is much easier to move on to more complex statistical techniques.

There are many different reasons why people say they feel they are bad at maths. For some, maths anxiety sets in early on and resistance to further learning becomes ingrained. In some cases, the poor quality of maths teaching is a significant factor. However, it would be unwise to overlook the proposition that maths is a more difficult subject to master than literacy-based ones. There is evidence for this from the 1870s and 1880s, when part of the funding provided to elementary schools in Victorian Britain was based on payment by results (Mitch, 2010). It was very clear from the payments made to schools based on standardised testing of pupils by inspectors that, in general, reading and writing were being taught more successfully than arithmetic. For example, Mitch cites a report from 1867 that gives the average pass rates in Church of England schools across the country as being 89 per cent for reading, 85.2 per cent for writing and 73.8 per cent for arithmetic. This is a common pattern in that it is repeated over time and across wide geographical areas.

Another reason some children find maths very challenging in the early years is that it requires a great deal of factual learning, whether that be of the times tables or the rules governing basic arithmetical procedures. For example, an adult would find it easy to divide 6 by 2. However, if asked to divide 716 by 5 as a mental arithmetic

problem the task becomes much more demanding. You
not only have to recall the rules for carrying out division,
but also to remember all the numbers as you work your
way through each step of the process. It also requires
drawing on long term memory – which may have become
rather rusty through lack of practice – as well as a good
working memory capacity. I recall the occasion when a
maths teacher told me she could not work this question
out without writing it down. There is a reasonable body
of evidence (e.g. Friso-van der Bos *et al.*, 2013) showing
a strong link between working memory and doing well
at arithmetic. Passolunghi and Lanfranchi (2011) also
report a strong relationship between processing speed and
numerical competence in 6-year old pupils. They conclude
that children who are 'poor in these general cognitive skills
[working memory and processing speed] may be particularly
disadvantaged in school, given that these skills appear to
be crucial, particularly at the early stage of mathematics
learning' (p59). As a working memory deficit and a slow
processing speed are frequently recorded when dyslexia,
dyspraxia or ADHD is present, many individuals with these
specific learning differences report having some difficulties
with arithmetic in their early school years.

For example, Samantha, a biochemistry student with
a diagnosis of dyslexia, struggled to learn the times tables
and described herself as being 'pretty poor' at mental
arithmetic. However, she pointed out she was 'much better
at algebra'. Samantha felt the description of herself as
finding easy maths difficult but difficult maths (e.g. algebra,
calculus) easy was quite apt. Her test profile revealed a

significant working memory deficit and, in spite of a strong mathematical background, her performance on a test of mental arithmetic was only average. This does not mean she is poor at maths. Instead, in Samantha's case, it illustrates the limitations imposed by her working memory deficit.

Sanjit has a diagnosis of dyspraxia with ADHD. When I met him he was studying maths at a prestigious university. He described himself as being 'reasonable to poor' at maths at primary school. When asked about his experience of learning the times tables he replied, 'I don't learn lists well'. He struggled with mental arithmetic and much prefers to write calculations down. However, in high school Sanjit excelled at maths. Like Samantha, his test profile reveals a major working memory deficit and he is a classic example of someone who finds easy maths difficult but difficult maths easy.

It is important to avoid assuming that everyone who has a working memory deficit will struggle with arithmetic. Layla, who has a diagnosis of ADHD, recalled enjoying maths at school and being 'the fastest in the class' at mental arithmetic. In spite of being poor at remembering sequences of numbers (a measure of working memory) she was exceptionally good at mental arithmetic. On being asked about the strategies she employs when engaged in mental arithmetic, Layla said she can 'see' the calculations when undertaking multiplications and long division. To calculate a percentage she converts the numbers to fractions and then simplifies them. (NB: This is a very unusual way of arriving at a percentage.) It is as if each stage is visually laid over the previous one and she has a mental blackboard on which she can 'see' the numbers and her workings out.

Both Samantha and Sanjit are very competent at maths and can work things out from first principles. However, memorising facts and procedures is a challenge for them. In spite of their under-performing on tests of mental arithmetic it would be very misleading to therefore conclude that they are 'bad at maths'. Whenever I give someone a standardised maths test, once they have completed it I look over their answers with them and ask what they found easy and what they found hard. It is often the case that when a working memory deficit is present some questions will have been avoided because they have forgotten the procedures for carrying out long division and multiplication, or how to solve questions with fractions. However, they often manage to answer most of the algebraic questions correctly.

The key point is that a low score on a maths test does not necessarily mean that someone is poor at maths. A low score can be due to many different factors (Moody, 2016). For example, if the test is time-limited a low score may reflect a slow speed of working. Inattention can also play a part. When ADHD is present it is not uncommon to observe errors on simple questions but a better performance on more difficult ones. It is as if, when a maths problem becomes more challenging, some individuals become much more focused and their error rate decreases. Scores from maths tests can be misleading if they are accepted uncritically, so it is vital to place them in the wider context of an individual's maths history.

The fifth edition of the DSM (Diagnostic and Statistical Manual of Mental Disorders) has introduced a different assessment philosophy from the approach specified in the fourth edition. In the earlier edition a diagnosis of maths impairment was dependent on recording a significant disparity between a Fullscale IQ score and a much lower score on a standardised test of maths. This was far too loose a definition, for there are many standardised tests of maths and these often measure different sets of mathematical skills. The use of Full Scale IQ (see Chapter 1) as a comparative measure is also to be discouraged. DSM-5 introduces a major change in assessment philosophy, with the purpose no longer being diagnosis but instead intervention.

In addition to emphasising the need to take a detailed history of educational skills, it is necessary to place scores for maths tests within the context of other educational skills. There should also be an emphasis on identifying what form the maths difficulty or difficulties take. If a decision is reached that a maths weakness is present, the recommended diagnosis is 'specific learning disorder with impairment in mathematics'. Possible forms of maths deficit include:

- number sense;
- memorisation of arithmetic facts;
- accurate or fluent calculation;
- accurate mathematical reasoning.

Only the first of these, number sense, should be classified as dyscalculia. Brian Butterworth, generally recognised as one of the foremost experts on dyscalculia, is very clear on the need to avoid confusing dyscalculia with maths impairment and he has proposed that the core deficit of dyscalculia is a lack of numerosity i.e. the inability to understand the concept of 'more than/less than' (Butterworth, 2013). For example, if you were to look at two photographs, one of which features two people and the other four people, without having to count you would instantly be able to know how many people there are in each photograph and thus which one includes more than the other. This ability to automatically arrive at an accurate number without counting is called subitisation, and it is usually restricted to numbers up to 4.

This is a very basic cognitive process and is recognised as being an innate ability that many other species have. The evolutionary advantage would appear to be obvious. If you are out-numbered you avoid conflict. However, when dyscalculia is present this very basis skill is absent or badly impaired. If you are unable to say which of two groups of objects or symbols is the larger, then learning the magnitudes assigned by numbers (e.g. 3 is half of 6) will be almost impossible. If numbers have little or no meaning, then very basic arithmetical processes, such as addition and subtraction, will be completely baffling. These very serious consequences for developing maths skills led Landerl *et al.* (2004) to conclude 'individuals who lack this sense of numerosity will have problems with even the most basic functions involving numbers such as subitising, counting small numbers of objects, using number names and numerals, and comparing numerical magnitudes, as well as more advanced arithmetical skills.' Their research is also important in demonstrating that dyscalculia is not linked to either reading ability or working memory. In their words, 'dyscalculia is the result of specific disabilities in basic numerical processing, rather than the consequence of deficits in other cognitive abilities' (p99).

Probably the best estimate of the proportion of individuals who are dyscalculic comes from a large-scale study carried out in Havana (Reigosa-Crespo *et al.*, 2011). They identified just over 9 per cent of the children in their survey as having a maths weakness (referred to as arithmetical dysfluency), with about a third of these (3.4 per cent) being dyscalculic. Interestingly, whereas the majority of the dyscalculic pupils were boys, the balance between girls and boys was close to being even for those with a maths weakness.

I have been aware for some years of the need to distinguish between individuals with what I refer to as a specific maths weakness and those who are dyscalculic and have developed my own screening test for dyscalculia. Some of the questions assess numerosity by requiring four numbers (e.g. 11,973; 8,752; 10,484; 9,515) to be arranged into ascending order and others assess understanding of the concept of 'more than/less than' with respect to percentages and ratios. For example, 'If David attends lectures on 53 per cent of occasions, Ravi's attendance is 92 per cent and Emily attends lectures on 78 per cent of occasions, who has the best attendance record and who the worst?'.

To my surprise I have yet to arrive at a diagnosis of dyscalculia. As almost all the individuals I see are university students or adults in professional employment,

it may be the case that being dyscalculic is so disabling
it results in most never being able to meet the maths
requirements set by many universities. However, I do see
individuals who have a specific maths weakness. Elma is a
music student with ADHD who has always struggled with
maths. She had difficulties with mental arithmetic and
learning the times tables, and also struggled with addition
and subtraction. This is a problem when she is working
in retail, 'I always give the wrong change. Having to cash
up is a nightmare.' She said she has 'developed a fear of
numbers'. When I read out a short series of numbers to
Elma she 'saw' the numbers rush up to her face, which
she found intimidating. It was obvious maths anxiety is a
significant factor for her.

When Elma was sixteen she sat a number of high
school exams (known in the UK as GCSEs – General
Certificate of Secondary Education). She achieved an
A grade for Music, B for English language and French,
but E for maths. On my screening test she correctly
answered all the questions requiring an understanding of
the concept of 'more than/less than' but made mistakes
on simple questions involving subtraction, division and
multiplication. Her performance on a standardised test of
maths was low – in the bottom 16 per cent. However, her
reading and spelling skills were in line with expectations
(see Figure 5.1). In terms of her neurocognitive profile
Elma's lowest score was for visual reasoning skills and I
would expect this to result in difficulties with those aspects
of maths, such as geometry, that require visual reasoning
skills. However, this would not account for the totality of

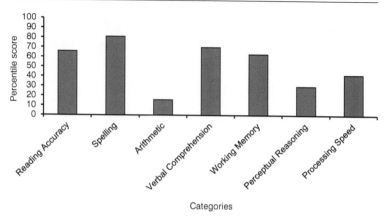

Categories

Figure 5.1 Elma's profile

Elma's maths difficulties. Even though there were a number of factors that contributed to Elma's maths difficulties (e.g. maths anxiety, working memory deficit), these were not sufficient to fully account for her long-standing difficulties. A diagnosis of specific maths weakness was justified.

Ruby, like Elma, dropped maths as soon as she could. Her difficulties with maths were obvious from early on and her parents paid for her to have private maths tutoring while she was at primary and secondary school. At secondary school Ruby was placed in the top groups for history and geography, and the bottom groups for maths and languages. Even though she just failed to pass her maths exam when she was sixteen, her mark was still, in her eyes, an excellent one. When asked about her experience of learning the times tables Ruby replied 'because of repetition, it was easier than the other aspects of maths'. She was prone to transposing numbers (e.g. misreading 54 as 45) and she still does this with telephone numbers. When she goes shopping she keeps track of her expenses by rounding everything up to the nearest pound, e.g. an item costing 47 pence will be mentally costed at one pound. Ruby mentioned she prefers buying fruit and vegetables from market stalls where all the scoops are priced at one pound.

Ruby was first diagnosed as being dyslexic when she was an undergraduate studying sociology. Although it was a struggle she successfully graduated and gained employment with a large law firm. After a few years of gaining experience of the range of work undertaken by this company, Ruby was appointed to a post which required her to spend most of her time auditing accounts. This was very repetitive work and also very numerical. Ruby became concerned about the errors she was making, such as missing out decimal points, transposing numbers and misreading statements. When she asked for advice on how she could improve the quality of her work, Ruby's employers referred her for a diagnostic assessment as there was a concern she might be dyscalculic.

Ruby's assessment confirmed her previous diagnosis of dyslexia and also revealed she is dyspraxic. Her neurocognitive profile (see Figure 5.2) is a typically spiky one. The presence of her working memory deficit would, by itself, account for some of her early difficulties with arithmetic at school. However, I have come across mathematicians who have dyslexia or dyspraxia, and so being dyslexic or dyspraxic is not, in itself, a causal factor for maths impairment.

Ruby is able to understand the concept of 'more than/less than', so she is not dyscalculic. However, her

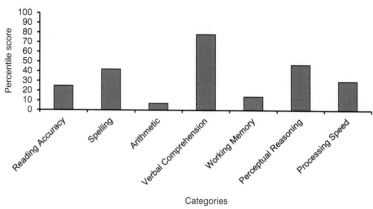

Figure 5.2 Ruby's profile

performance on a standardised test of maths ability was
very weak across a wide range of skills (e.g. percentages,
fractions, division, subtraction, algebra) and her test score
placed her in the bottom 7 per cent for her age group.
As her history revealed a long and continuing history
of maths difficulties, in spite of private tutoring when
she was at school, a diagnosis of specific maths weakness
('impairment in maths', if you prefer the American
diagnostic classification) was justified. As a consequence
of her diagnosis her company was able to transfer her to a
post that did not require numerical skills.

In everyday life Ruby will continue to struggle with
the wide range of activities that require basic numerical
abilities, such as shopping, cooking, estimating time to
get to a destination, working out postage or converting
currency on holiday. However, she was fortunate in being
employed by a company that took seriously its obligations
to make appropriate work adjustments for employees
with specific learning differences. In spite of technology

making it easier to answer numerical questions, there is no escaping the multiple ways in which basic numerical skills are important in everyday life and at work.

References

Butterworth, B. (2013) Dyscalculia. Talk given at Richmond upon Thames College to members of the Dyslexia Network, June 24.

Friso-van der Bos, I., van der Ven, S.H.G., Kroesbergen, E.H., & van Lui, J.E.H. (2013) Working memory and mathematics in primary school children: A meta-analysis. *Education Research Review*, 10: 29–44.

Landerl, K., Bevan, A., & Butterworth, B. (2004) Developmental dyscalculia and basic numerical capacities: a study of 8–9-year-old students. *Cognition*, 93: 99–125.

Mitch, D. (2010) Education funding in Victorian Britain: 'Payment by results' boosted pupil achievement. Paper presented at the Economic History Society's 2010 annual conference.

Moody, S. (2016) Maths and number difficulties: A close analysis. *PATOSS Bulletin*, 29 (1): 36–39.

Passolunghi, M.C., & Lanfranchi, S. (2011) Domain-specific and domain-general precursors of mathematical achievement: A longitudinal study from kindergarten to first grade. *British Journal of Developmental Psychology*, 82: 42–63.

Reigosa-Crespo, V., Valdés-Sosa, M., Butterworth, B., Estévez, N., Rodríguez, M., Santos, E., Torres, P., Suárez, R., & Lage, A. (2011) Basic numerical capacities and prevalence of developmental dyscalculia: The Havana survey. *Developmental Psychology*, 48 (1): 1–13.

Chapter 6

Visualisation and synaesthesia

It was late morning on a late Spring day. Jasmine, free of work pressures, had enjoyed a long lie-in. The sun was shining and already she could feel its warmth as it streamed through her window. Taking her time to get dressed she decided to take a walk in her local park while thinking where to go for a coffee and a late breakfast. Walking through the park gates she stopped for a moment to admire the vibrant colour of the tulips and their delicate scent. Walking on, she strolled for a short while alongside the park lake. Several couples were already out rowing on the lake and their laughter mingled with the sound of the gentle waves lapping by her feet. There was a whoosh as a lycra-clad cyclist sped past. A spaniel padded up to her and she bent down to tickle it behind its floppy ears. After a few seconds of enjoying being petted it bounced away to join its owner. Having then spotted a café in the distance Jasmine quickened her steps. It was now time for a coffee.

When reading about Jasmine, how did you experience the act of reading? Was it as if you were just hearing the words being spoken in your mind, or did you start to create a mental image of Jasmine? Or a combination of both? My own experience of reading is as mentally hearing the words being spoken. On occasions, when skim-reading, it is as if I sense the meaning of the words. Other people report very different experiences. Without having to think how she does it, Camila, who has ADHD, creates mental pictures of what she is reading. By the time she had finished reading the above passage Camila's 'mind's eye' image of Jasmine was very detailed:

> Jasmine is a delicate female with long flowing brown hair. She likes to wear very country colours and long dresses that hug her slender frame with comfort and ease. Although she doesn't wear make-up, every now and again she likes to decorate her plum soft lips with a red tint, a rather bold look in comparison to her softly spoken manner.

John, who is dyslexic, developed quite a different image and reported 'seeing' Jasmine as being 'an upper-class woman with dark brown/black hair, naturally light brown skin, hair half way down her back, red lips, thin toned woman, stylish, expensive clothes (white skinny jeans)'. Tracy, who has a diagnosis of both ADHD and dyspraxia, described Jasmine as having 'long blonde hair. She is wearing a flower print dress and a pair of plain black shoes, and she is carrying a phone in her right hand'.

In spite of reading exactly the same set of words, Camila, John and Tracy arrived at strikingly different visual impressions of Jasmine. For those individuals who are able to visualise a story when reading it is not surprising that, when watching a film of a book they have read, they are often disappointed, 'It is not how I saw it'. For those individuals who do experience strong visualisation when reading, what can be considered a bonus is that their recall of what they have just read is usually very visual as well, 'Like watching a TV programme'.

However, not all books are easily visualised. Whereas Camila's visualisation when reading a fiction book for enjoyment is very strong, this is not the case for academic texts. When experiencing a text 'just as words', with no accompanying images, she finds reading for meaning 'just so hard ... I need images to understand'. Like many individuals with dyslexia, dyspraxia or ADHD, Camila's working memory capacity is quite limited, which makes it very difficult to remember academic, fact-intensive material without the support of accompanying images. This applies to other facets of her life as well. Because she has a strong visual memory, she is very good at remembering faces. However, her difficulty with remembering names is often a source of embarrassment to her.

The ability to visualise varies significantly, not only from person to person but also from activity to activity. The likely incidence and intensity of visualisation also varies with which specific learning difference, or combination of specific learning differences, is present. This phenomenon is explored later in this chapter.

Camila, who has ADHD, is representative of the minority of individuals who experience vivid visualisation, including synaesthesia, in response to a wide range of stimuli. For example, when a sequence of words was read out, each of them evoked an instant image for her. She described how, on hearing the word *giraffe*, she instantly 'saw' a mental picture of a giraffe in a zoo, and this then changed into one of the animal walking slowly across the savanna, as if in a David Attenborough television documentary. The name *Teresa* initially evoked an image of the 'historic Teresas'. She then reported being able to see all the historical Teresas and people she knew with that name 'all in the same room'. On being asked whether *Tuesday* conjured up an image or a colour, Camila replied *Tuesday* was orange/light brown. Other days of the week were different colours: *Monday* was yellow; *Wednesday* light purple; *Thursday* vibrant dark blue; and *Friday* burgundy/purple.

Camila said her day/colour combinations have never changed, '*Monday* has always been yellow', and so synaesthesia is said to be present. Synaesthesia is an involuntary blending of two or more senses (e.g. words and colours). Day/colour synaesthesia is reported as being probably the most common form of synaesthesia, with perhaps as many as 1 in 36 people experiencing it (Simner *et al.*, 2006). The key defining feature of synaesthesia is that an individual's associations must have been consistent over time. However, the particular combinations experienced in day/colour synaesthesia vary from person to person. For example, Oliver described *Monday* as being blue, *Tuesday* 'like the red of nicotine gum', *Wednesday* sky blue, *Thursday* lime-green and *Friday* as being 'post-box red'. There are times when the colour of a day is described with a high degree of precision, so a day is perceived as being not just blue but a particular hue or shade of blue such as azure, teal, turquoise or 'blue as the colour of the sky reflected in a puddle'.

Going back to 1881, Sir Francis Galton (the cousin of Charles Darwin) was making the same point:

The seers are invariably most minute in their description of the precise tint and hue of the colour. They are never satisfied, for instance, with saying 'blue,' but will take a great deal of trouble to express or to match the particular blue they mean. Lastly, no two people agree, or hardly ever do so, as to the colour they associate with the same sound (p 646).

Camila's day/colour synaesthesia, allied with her strong visualisation ability, enables her to create a mental visual calendar. She sees the days as a timetable with the days tinted in and mentioned she prefers a timetable to a diary. When she has made an appointment she places it on her mental calendar, almost like a post-it note, with the hour slots being colour-coded (e.g. 3 o'clock is green and 4 o'clock blue). While Camila's calendar visualisation may appear extraordinary, John's is even more so. When given the name *Catherine* he instantly replied he 'saw' the date 1991. This most unusual response was explored with him and he explained he has separate lines for days, months and years. These are all interlinked with specific memories of events – akin to video clips – mapped onto the relevant day, month and year. In addition to the days of the week having their own colours, the months are coloured as well. For example, *April* is 'spring green' and *August* 'harvest gold'. He pointed out he mentally experiences *March* and *September* as being 'windy'. He referred to this as being a 'multi-dimensional living map' that is constantly being updated. While John's exceptional visual memory means he is able to dip back in time for many years and recall an event as if viewing a video recording of it, like Camila there are times when his rich tapestry of concurrent verbal, visual and emotional thoughts results in sensory overload and he has to take time out to calm his brain down.

Some individuals not only experience mental pictures triggered by words but are able to 'see' the word in its written form as well. When this specific ability is reported the visualised words are usually similar to each other in terms of font and colour, such as black lower-case lettering on a white background. Occasionally an individual will report that each word, or each letter, has its own colour. This is another form of synaesthesia.

Florence, who is dyspraxic and has ADHD, identified her major concern as being a difficulty with writing essays. This was not surprising as essay writing is a common issue for individuals who are either dyspraxic or have ADHD. However, the source of her difficulties with essay writing was most unusual. She was studying Spanish at university and described herself as being good at spelling. On being taken through a short series of words she said she could 'see' each of them, with all the words being coloured: *Mary* was brown and pink; *John* orange; *Lima* yellow; *Madrid* purple; and *rabbit* brown. Florence pointed out most letters have their own colour (e.g. *a* light green, *b* blue, *m* purple, *j* orange, *c* orange). In general, the first letter of a word determines the colour of the rest of the word, except when a letter has a particularly dominant colour. She gave as an example of this her own name. She said '*Florence* is "overall blue", but *l* adds a splash of yellow'. Florence's word/colour associations impact on her writing in that the combination of colours she experiences when creating a page of text has to be harmonious. This is also an important factor when undertaking translations in that she tries to find appropriate words that do not have clashing colours. As a consequence, her attempts to achieve a harmonious balance of colours leads to slowness mixed with frustration when writing and undertaking translation.

One of the twentieth century's greatest physicists, Richard Feynman (1980, p.59), had letter/colour synaesthesia:

> When I see equations, I see the letters in colors – I don't know why. As I'm talking, I see vague pictures of Bessel functions from Jahnke and Emde's book, with light-tan j's, slightly violet-bluish n's, and dark brown x's flying around. And I wonder what the hell it must look like to the students.

Feynman's comment, 'I don't know why', reveals he was not aware he was a synaesthete. This is often the case, for many individuals with strong visualisation abilities and/ or synaesthesia frequently believe the way they perceive the world is no different from that of other people. In my experience this is the case even when the type of synaesthesia is quite unusual.

Perhaps the rarest form of word-based synaesthesia is ticker-tape synaesthesia. Harry, who is dyspraxic with ADHD, described how, when he is talking or being spoken to, 'I see the words scrolling across [from left to right] … It's as if I'm reading an autocue'. When he was given an unfamiliar word, *tachistoscope*, he 'saw' it in bold white letters and had no difficulty spelling it. Luke's ticker-tape synaesthesia was slightly different. (Luke has a specific language impairment.) He said it only occurs when he is listening to the radio and not doing anything else. If this is the case, 'each word just pops up'. For both Harry and Luke, it was only when they were asked about their visualisation abilities that they became aware for the first time they were synaesthetes.

While ticker-tape synaesthesia is very rare, the ability to 'see' numbers, days, months and the alphabet in spatial form, such as a line or circle, is much more common, and one estimation is that about 20 per cent of the population may have this ability. Perhaps the earliest description of someone with the ability to mentally 'see' numbers arranged in a line dates from 1873. This was mentioned in 1880 by Sir Francis Galton when he provided numerous accounts (with diagrams) of many individuals' visualisation of numbers. He gives several accounts of people with the ability to solve mental arithmetic problems as if viewing a mental backboard, on which both the numbers and workings-out were written. There is also a report of number/colour synaesthesia (for example, one individual perceived 3 as being yellow, 4 red, 5 greenish-yellow and 6 was blue).

Galton's paper also includes what is probably the first account of what is now called ordinal-linguistic personification synaesthesia. In this form of synaesthesia numbers have personalities. Galton gives the example of an individual with this form of synaesthesia describing 1 as being 'a common-place drudge', 2 as 'young and sprightly', and 9 as 'a wonderful being of whom I felt almost afraid' (p253). While this form of synaesthesia is, in my experience, very rare, I do occasionally meet people for whom numbers have personalities. Mark, an Economics student who has ADHD, told me that numbers 'have very strong personalities'. For him, even numbers are usually very sharp and odd numbers very soft.

On being taken through a series of numbers he described 8 as being a number he dislikes, 'it's too fierce'; 9 is 'very friendly, soft'; 2 is a number he has always liked; 4 is boring; 5 is soft but 'always wrong'; 7 is 'really strong, a happy number'. Because numbers have personalities, his selection of a pin number is determined by whether he is comfortable with all the digits. Perhaps unsurprisingly, his ability to visualise numbers was exceptionally strong and he gave as an example being able to visualise matrix problems. (A matrix is a grid of numbers.) He mentioned he was particularly strong at maths.

The question of whether the ability to visualise is advantageous is an interesting one. For example, there is a claim (Ward et al., 2008) that 'Synaesthetes experiencing vision from music are far more likely to play an instrument than their other synaesthetic counterparts.' Anton is a dyslexic music student (piano) and Nadia is a dyspraxic music student (violin). Both are music synaesthetes. Anton said that when he is playing he is 'looking for the colour in the music'. His colours are linked to chords and he gave as examples F major being orange, B flat major purple, D major green, E major bright yellow, with the minor chords being grey. Unlike Anton, Nadia was already aware of being a music synaesthete. Nadia's colours are linked to notes and she gave as examples C being grey, D brown, E light blue, F sharp light green and B flat burgundy. As an aid to reading a musical score, Nadia spends hours colour-coding the manuscript.

Anton and Nadia are in good company. Well known music synaesthetes include Franz Liszt, Jean Sibelius, David Hockney and Duke Ellington. There is also some evidence that Bob Dylan is a music synaesthete: 'I don't know if I call myself a poet or not.... It's more of a visual type of thing for me. I could picture the color of the song' … 'It's that wild mercury sound. It's metallic and bright gold, whatever that conjures up.'

In my experience, music synaesthesia can take different forms. James, a dyslexic commercial music student, described how, when trying to work out the structure of a piece of music, he experiences it as a combination of shapes and colours. For example, harsh percussion gives rise to red squares and a saxophone or flute creates 'soft, more fluid shapes'. He generally experiences the bass as a blue colour. Mimi, a history of art student with ADHD, experiences dance and classical music as colours and patterns. When listening to New York is Killing Me (a techno piece of music), she can 'see' two grid patterns moving towards each other. The sections within the grids are coloured. As the two grids pass through each other the colours alter but then change back to their original colour as the grids separate.

Not everyone experiences imagery while listening to music and even fewer are music synaesthetes. When music is reported as being associated with the creation of mental pictures, these images tend to take one of two forms. For some, a piece of music immediately evokes a visual memory of where they were when they first heard that piece of music, whereas others report a more creative form of imagery in that they either make up their own story, often akin to a pop video, or imagine themselves as a member of the band, orchestra or dance troupe.

For many individuals the visual vividness of their everyday thinking and memories is fundamental to how they learn, how they experience the past and the present and think about the future, and to being creative. This should not be surprising, for in evolutionary terms the ability to recall visual memories and create new mental images has to predate the development of language. It is no accident that the technique of the ancient Greeks to remember a sequence of events when telling a story is based on using visual clues as triggers for specific parts of the narrative. It is as if a more recent skill – in evolutionary terms – (language) is being superimposed on a more ancient and enduring skill (visualisation).

What is surprising, given the centrality of visualisation to so many, is how little we know about it. Linda Phillips and her colleagues (2010) refer to the 'dearth of research and scholarship on visualisations'. For example, if we ask how many people experience visualisation when reading, the simple answer is 'we don't know'. This lack of awareness and understanding about visualisation results in significant difficulties when confronted with the statement, 'Many dyslexic people are gifted at seeing

Illustration 6.1

things in the mind's eye' (Brunswick, 2012, p199). As visualisation varies both from activity to activity and from person to person, it is necessary to specify both the form of the visualisation and the comparison groups.

For many years now, when carrying out a diagnostic assessment, I have asked individuals to rate the quality of their visualisation when reading for pleasure using a rating scale from 1 (no visualisation) to 5 (images in high definition and colour). As I needed a neurotypical comparison group I commissioned a survey at Leeds Metropolitan University. Of the 76 students with no diagnosis of a specific learning difference, 67 per cent reported experiencing visualisation when reading. However, in a number of cases this was at a low or moderate level. When the neurotypical group was divided into those with high or low levels of visualisation, the subgroup sizes were very similar – about 40 per cent in each case. This is also the case for the dyspraxics I have seen, in that 36 per cent report a low level of visualisation and 32 per cent strong visualisation.

If it is the case that dyslexics are visual thinkers, it would be anticipated that more dyslexics would experience a high level of visualisation when reading than neurotypicals. Although there is a shift in that direction (28 per cent of dyslexics being low visualisers vs. 42 per cent high visualisers – a ratio of 1.5), it is only a minor one, and it is well below that recorded for individuals with ADHD, of whom just 14 per cent were in the low visualisation group while 51 per cent were in the high one. That is, a ratio of

3.6 high visualisers to every 1 who reported a low level of visualisation.

While this may be a surprising outcome, I have also found synaesthetic experiences are reported more frequently by individuals with ADHD than by dyslexics: 17 per cent compared with 9 per cent. Intriguingly, 14 per cent of dyspraxics also report synaesthetic experiences. When dyspraxia and ADHD co-occur, the incidence of synaesthesia shoots up to 37 per cent. However, this is not the case when dyslexia and ADHD co-occur, for the incidence of synaesthesia is 18 per cent. This figure is virtually the same as when ADHD is the only diagnosis. At the risk of being controversial, it appears to me that visualisation is at its highest when ADHD is present, but – and it is an important but – not all individuals with ADHD report a high level of visualisation. This is even more true for dyslexics.

In what is considered to be the best controlled survey looking at the prevalence of synaesthesia (Simner et al., 2006), the researchers report that 4.4 per cent of the adult population are synaesthetes, with day–colour synaesthesia being the most common, followed by grapheme–colour synaesthesia. I have also found day–colour synaesthesia to be the most commonly reported type of synaesthesia. While the proportion of individuals with specific learning differences reporting synaesthetic experiences is noticeably higher than that reported by Simner et al. for a neurotypical population, this is not unexpected given that their survey set quite demanding standards to ensure the genuine presence of synaesthesia. What is important about my data is the clear link between different specific learning differences and the incidence of synaesthesia.

I was not surprised to record a higher frequency of synaesthesia for individuals with ADHD than for those with dyslexia or dyspraxia given that lack of inhibition is a classic ADHD feature, and there are some researchers who attribute synaesthesia to a lack of inhibition at a neuronal level. It is as if some neural networks do not have sufficient insulation to inhibit cross-talk between networks and so cortical excitability can be higher than for a neurotypical individual. I have also come to appreciate that hypersensitivity is a typical ADHD experience. It is as if some neuronal circuits require very little in the way of stimuli to trigger a reaction. Therefore, these circuits may pick up activity in networks close by that would not be sensed by a neurotypical individual. A combination of hypersensitivity and lack of inhibition could potentially account for the greater incidence of synaesthesia in individuals with ADHD.

The link between synaesthesia and dyspraxia would appear to be more puzzling, but it may reflect a link between hypersensitivity and the size of adjacent brain areas. In recent years it has been shown that synaesthetes have finer colour discrimination than control groups, with this greater sensitivity being linked to a visual pathway in the brain. However, this sensitivity, which requires rather more brain space, appears to be associated with reduced sensitivity in a neuronal pathway linked with motion detection (Bannisy et al., 2012). As poor motor coordination is a defining feature of dyspraxia, this may be reflected in some subtle damage to motor pathways in the brain, which in turn permits an adjacent area to expand and become hyper-sensitive.

There is much we don't yet know about either visualisation or synaesthesia, including their role in being creative. Intuitively, it would appear to be an essential skill for a wide range of professions including fashion, design, art, and film and television directing and producing. For example, Alessandro Michele, Gucci Design Director, when asked about his 2015 Autumn fashion show, replied, 'I try to map out what is in my head'. At the opening of an exhibition of her 2009 exhibition, *Those Who Suffer Love*, the famous British artist Tracey Emin, who is probably dyslexic, said 'I am the custodian, the curator of the images that live in my mind'. Kajol, a Bollywood superstar, when asked why she sometimes turns down a film role that others feel would be an excellent one for her, replied, 'If I can't feel a character, if I can't visualise that, then I'm not the right person for it'. Tony Gordon, television scriptwriter and creator and lead writer on the series *Dickensian*, referred to his source of inspiration for *Dickensian* as having 'This idea in my mind of an urchin boy with his face pressed up against a window looking through the glass at a big man inside, warm with a ham and a glass of port.'

Not everyone has the ability to visualise. In 2015, Zeman *et al.* reported on a group of individuals who scored very low on the Vividness of Visual Imagery Questionnaire. These individuals reported a life-long condition of never being able to voluntarily visualise, a condition Zeman *et al.* suggested should be termed 'congenital aphantasia'. (NB:

The word *phantasia* was first used by the Greek philosopher Aristotle to describe imagination as the process by which we experience mental images.) While two-thirds of those with aphantasia in Zeman's reported difficulties with autobiographical memory, they also identified themselves as having strengths in the 'verbal, mathematical and logical domains'. While further work is required to demonstrate that this is the case there is very recent evidence that some artists and actors are aphantasic.

Susan Aldworth, an experimental printmaker and filmmaker, has interviewed a small number of professional practising artists (2016) about their use of visual imagination when creating art works. Unexpectedly, and in spite of being professionally successful, a number reported they do not have a visual imagination. Shaun May (2016), an actor and theatre director, has aphantasia, and describes this as being 'a disabling barrier in actor training', for a central tenant of the training of actors is that they must be able to draw upon their images in their 'mind's eye' when developing and performing a role. He poses the question of what would constitute a reasonable adjustment in actor training practices for those with low visual imagery.

There are claims visualisation skills can be taught, and this is a key belief underpinning the Lindamood-Bell teaching strategy for improving reading and comprehension skills of children with a range of specific learning differences, from dyslexia to ADHD to autism (Worthington, 2014). Not only do Paul Worthington and Nanci Bell (2016) claim 'individuals can be taught to consciously generate visual images, resulting in significant gains in reading and language comprehension', they also claim this is accompanied by neurological change as well. As aphantasia is such a new concept there is much work to be done to ascertain whether aphantasics can be taught visualisation skills, and to what advantage.

Perhaps the last word should go to Nadia. She is dyslexic and has ADHD and she has developed a passionate interest in playing Korean music. (It helps her run off excess energy.) Her level of visualisation is very high. When reading, Nadia said 'I see the whole thing play out in my head'. While listening to House music she experiences it as frequency waves, the colour of which is dependent on emotion. Relaxed emotions are yellow or bright neon green, while hectic ones are shades of blue and grey. Like many individuals with ADHD she was prone to daydreaming as a child and this is still the case. Nadia described daydreaming as being 'fun', adding 'I get my most creative ideas from daydreaming'.

References

Aldworth, S. (2016) The art of imagination. Paper presented at the international conference, The Eye's Mind: Visual Imagination, Neuroscience and the Humanities. University of East Anglia, UK, May 21–22, 2016.

Banissy, M.J., Tester, V., Muggleton, N.G., Janik, A.B., Davenport, A., Franklin, A., Walsh, V. & Ward, J. (2013) Synesthesia for color is linked to improved color perception but reduced motion perception. *Psychological Science*, 24: 2390–2397. Available at http://pss.sagepub.com/content/24/12/2390.full.pdf

Brunswick, N. (Ed) (2012) *Supporting Dyslexic Adults in Higher Education and the Workplace.* Wiley-Blackwell, Chichester.

Feynman, R. (1988) *What Do You Care What Other People Think? Further Adventures of a Curious Character.* Norton, New York.

Galton, F. (1880) Visualised numerals. *Nature*, 21: 252–256.

Galton, F. (1881) The visons of sane persons. *Proceedings of the Royal Institution*, 9: 644–655.

May, S. (2016) Visual imagination in actor training: The importance of the 'Minds' Eye' and the challenge of aphantasia. Paper presented at the international conference, The Eye's Mind: Visual Imagination, Neuroscience and the Humanities. University of East Anglia, May 21–22, 2016.

Phillips, L.M., Norris, S.P., & Macnab, J.S. (2010) *Visualisation in Mathematics, Reading and Science Education*, Springer, New York.

Simner, J., Mulvenna, C., Sagiv, N., Tsakanikos, E., Witherby, S.A., Fraser, C., Scott, K., & Ward, J. (2006) Synaesthesia: The prevalence of atypical cross-modal experiences. *Perception*, 35: 1024–1033.

Ward, J., Thompson-Lake, D., Ely, R., & Kaminski, F. (2008) Synaesthesia, creativity and art: What is the link? *British Journal of Psychology*, 99: 127–141.

Worthington, P. (2014) Learning difficulties: Symptoms, causes, and solutions. Proceedings of Braga 2014 Embracing Inclusive Approaches for Children and Youth with Special Education Needs Conference.

Worthington, P., & Bell, N. (2016) Visual Imagery: The nonverbal code for language and cognition. Paper presented at the international conference, The Eye's Mind: Visual Imagination, Neuroscience and the Humanities. University of East Anglia, May 21–22, 2016.

Zeman, A., Dewar, M., & Sala, S.D. (2015) Lives without imagery – congenital aphantasia. *Cortex*, 73: 378–380.

Further reading

Ward, J. (2008) *The Frog Who Croaked Blue. Synesthesia and the Mixing of the Senses.* Routledge, London & New York.

Chapter 7

Colours and reading

When Jack placed a transparent, pink-coloured plastic sheet over a page of text, to his surprise it stopped the words from 'floating about'. Just as astonishing was that, on reading the text aloud, his speed of reading increased by 65 per cent and he was then able to read at the speed of a non-dyslexic adult. Jack said he did not read a book from cover to cover until he was in his late teens, as at that time he had been remanded in custody and had nothing else to do. In his thirties Jack was diagnosed as being dyslexic and dyspraxic. A high level of visual stress was also present.

Visual stress is the name given to the experience some people have of visual distortions when looking at a page of text. When I look at a page all the words are clearly defined, they do not move and they all lie flat on the paper. The same is true when I look at a sheet of music. If visual stress is present, very different experiences are reported. For example, when Ellen looked at a page of text she described the words as looking 'like a lot of ants'. However, placing a rose-coloured overlay on the page 'killed the ants' and the words became 'settled and calm'. Furthermore, she could see 'an ocean of words'. When taken through a range of differently coloured overlays she chose the rose-coloured one as being the best in terms of improving her perception of the page of text. Using this overlay increased her reading speed by 22 per cent. Ellen is dyspraxic and has ADHD. She is prone to developing a migraine when she begins to read a book or academic paper and also becomes tired quite quickly when reading. After taking to wearing spectacles with rose-tinted lenses the frequency of her migraines decreased and she also found her ability to read the text in PowerPoint presentations in lectures improved.

Halima, a medical student, was first diagnosed as being dyslexic in the first year of her course. Multiple choice question (MCQ) tests are a key form of assessment in medical degrees and they require an ability to read with accuracy and a high level of fluency. Halima found herself unable to complete more than about 60 per cent of the first MCQ tests she sat. On being screened for visual stress her speed of reading increased by 30 per cent when using a lime-green overlay. Instead of the words 'meshing into each other' they now 'looked ordered'. By having the MCQ tests printed on suitably coloured paper, Halima was able to answer more of the questions. As she is dyslexic she also qualified for additional time in exams.

Visual stress is not a specific learning difference. It is rather like being short-sighted in that it results in a visual distortion but, unlike short-sightedness, the distortion occurs within the visual pathways of the brain rather than being due to the distortion of the curvature of the lens of the eye. Just as short-sightedness can be corrected by being prescribed the appropriate optical lens, so coloured overlays or tinted spectacle lenses can also correct visual stress. When visual stress is suspected it is best to consult a qualified optometrist who will also carry out a full optical examination. However, people sometimes find their own solutions such as using a highlighter, not just to mark important points or ideas in the text, but also because it makes the words easier to read. Others have taken to writing on yellow paper to avoid the white glare they experience when using white paper. One musician said he had taken to copying musical scores onto yellow paper. I remember being told by Peter Irons, one of the early assessors for visual stress, that he had met a boy who saved the purple transparent wrappings from Cadbury's Roses chocolates to place over words when reading.

In comparison with the main specific learning differences, which have a relatively long history, the first account of the use of coloured overlays to assist reading dates from 1964 when MacDonald Critchley described a case of a dyslexic child who was unable to read words on white card but could read from coloured card (Wilkins & Evans). Independently of each other, Oliver Meares in New Zealand (1980) and Helen Irlen in California (1983) reported that reading skills can be improved in some children through the use of coloured overlays or coloured paper (see Wilkins & Evans). For some time the visual disturbance they described was either referred to as Irlen Syndrome or Meares-Irlen Syndrome. More recently, the preferred term has become visual stress. For some years there was doubt about whether visual stress was a valid experience that could be offset through the use of coloured overlays or backgrounds. However, there is now much greater acceptance of the concept, even though we still do not fully understand why it occurs or why colours help.

There is also general acceptance visual stress is more likely to occur when dyslexia is present. About 50 per cent of the dyslexic individuals I have assessed also have visual stress, varying from quite mild to severe. That is, only a minority will significantly benefit from the use of coloured overlays. This is one reason why studies which have sought to examine the link between dyslexia and visual stress have been inconclusive. For example, Albon *et al.* (2008) conclude 'it remains a possibility that there exists a subgroup of people who may experience an improvement in reading through the use of coloured filters, while others find that there is no beneficial effect' (p8).

It has been suggested that dyslexia and visual stress are both due to a delay in visuo-temporal processing (Fisher *et al.*, 2015) that results from a magnocellular deficit. If this is so, it would be anticipated that this would be reflected in performance in sporting activities that require fast visuo-temporal processing. That is, someone who has both dyslexia and visual stress is unlikely to excel at sports. However, my 50 per cent figure also holds true for the thirty dyslexic elite sportspeople I refer to in Chapter 9. For example Ahmed, who has represented his county at cricket and won a silver medal in a national boxing competition, achieved a 30 per cent increase in reading speed by using a lime-green overlay. He was surprised that it made his field of focus much wider and 'the words look like words'. Claire, who had represented her county at hockey, golf and long jump, achieved a 20 per cent increase in reading speed using an aqua overlay. Without this overlay she described the text as looking like 'clumps of blocks'.

When visual stress is present it is important to identify the particular colour that is best for each individual. In my experience there is no one colour that is generally perceived as being the most beneficial. However, if the preferred colour is grey, this tends to indicate a general sensitivity to light. As I have recorded visual stress in about 10 per cent of ADHD individuals, and also in people with no history of having a specific learning difference, I am of the opinion that any assessment for a specific learning difference should include a screening for visual stress. There are grounds for recommending such a screening should also be carried out for anyone who suffers from frequent migraines.

Visual stress is strongest when the font size is small. This may be why it is not so obvious when a child first learns to read, as the font size is usually quite large. Once the print size is smaller and the horizontal and vertical lines that make up letters are much denser, the neuronal cells that differentially fire when exposed to vertical lines and lines that are close together start to create a noisy signal for the visual cortex (e.g. see Wilkins *et al.*, 2004). Within the visual pathways and the area of the brain that supports visual processing there are very specialised cells that only fire when a very specific visual detail presents itself. The anatomical arrangement of these cells is also very precise. For some people it is as if there is a hypersensitivity, which results in a kind of neuronal electrical overload and this then spills over into an adjacent area of the brain that is responsible for colour perception. As the colour cells are also very precisely arranged, this means the spill-over can affect areas relating to different colours, depending on precisely where in the neuronal pathway the spill-over occurs. The colour of the overlay that works best will be the one that damps down the area of spill-over. This may be why people sometimes find that, after a time, they need to change to a different coloured overlay, since when one area is damped down there is still a lesser spill-over into another part of the pathways.

Although there is much that is still not understood about why coloured overlays work, the reality is that for many people they do have a positive effect. Having observed an increase in reading speed of 65 per cent for Jack, the question that troubled me was that if he had been screened for visual stress when he was young, might his reading skills, in spite of him being dyslexic, have improved to the extent that he would have avoided a life of crime.

References

Albon, E., Adi, Y., & Hyde, C. (2008) *The Effectiveness and Cost-effectiveness of Coloured Filters for Reading Disability: A Systematic Review*. West Midlands Health Technology Assessment Collaboration. University of Birmingham. Report No 67.

Fisher, C., Chekaluk, E., & Irwin, J. (2015) Impaired driving performance as evidence of a magnocellular deficit in dyslexia and visual stress. *Dyslexia*, 21: 350–360.

Wilkins, A., Huang., J., & Cao, Y. (2004) Visual stress theory and its application to reading and reading tests. *Journal of Research in Reading*, 27 (2): 152–162.

Wilkins, A. & Evans, B. Visual stress and its treatment. Available at: www.essex.ac.uk/psychology/overlays/. Last accessed June 6, 2016.

Chapter 8

Being creative – or becoming creative?

How can we explain the preponderance of creativity and 'thinking outside the box' in many people with dyslexia?
(Maryann Wolf, 2008, p200).

If you Google 'famous dyslexics', the lists of names that pop up contain a high proportion of people from the creative industries, including artists, writers, film-makers, musicians and actors. While some of the frequently occurring names such as Walt Disney, Pablo Picasso, Albert Einstein and John Lennon are open to challenge, there are famous individuals such as Steven Spielberg, Nigel Kennedy and Jamie Oliver who have confirmed diagnoses of dyslexia. The linking of dyslexia with being creative is international: the Indian film 'Stars upon the Ground' features the story of a dyslexic child who is treated badly at home and school because of his dyslexia, but then goes on to succeed after his artistic talents are recognised by his art teacher.

What then is understood by the assertion that dyslexic individuals are generally more creative in their thinking than others and why might this be so? Is there something unique about the way dyslexics think that results in their being more creative than others? Jane Graves, a practising psychoanalytical psychotherapist with considerable experience of teaching and working with dyslexic students at Central Saint Martin's college of art and design, suggests that 'creativity comes into being when the unconscious comes into conflict with the conscious mind' (2007, p42). Aiding this process is the technique of free association, which Jane Graves claims is used by 'artists, designers, poets, novelists, [and] dancers' as a creative strategy. This technique, which enables 'thoughts and feelings to talk to each other', could be viewed as a key to 'thinking outside the box'. While 'thinking outside the box' is not unique to dyslexics, it could be argued that it is more likely to occur when dyslexia is present.

One of the consequences of being dyslexic is a tendency to give voice to a thought as soon as it comes to mind, to ensure it is not forgotten a few minutes later. This spontaneous expression of a seemingly unconnected idea conveys the impression of going off at a tangent that may be seen as akin to a stream of consciousness. Answers to questions may therefore be unexpected ones and appear to reflect 'thinking outside the box'. However, people with dyspraxia and/or particularly ADHD are, in my experience, equally likely to go off at tangents, so why are they not perceived as being just as creative as dyslexics?

More conventionally, Jane Graves also identifies visual-spatial ability – which she defines as an ability to 'judge visual information as a whole and to change view points in the mind' – as being a source of creativity for art and design students who are dyslexic. She is not alone in suggesting a visual ability link between dyslexia and creativity. Intuitively, a strength in visual reasoning skills would appear to be important for succeeding in art and design. Does it therefore follow that individuals with dyslexia are stronger at visual thinking than neurotypicals? However, it is not that simple. In 2010, Alexander-Passe, in the opening comments of a book he edited on dyslexia and creativity, offers the following comment, 'research to date has been unable to support the claim that dyslexics are creative or have visual-spatial talents in excess of the normal population'.

This conclusion does not surprise me. The creative process is a very complex one and cannot be attributed to a single factor. To begin with, it is necessary to define creativity and what form it may take. Being creative can be viewed as the ability to arrive at new or novel solutions that are effective. Note the emphasis on functionality. Secondly, it is highly likely that creativity takes different forms. For example, Kozhevnikov et al. (2013) refer to scientific creativity, artistic creativity and verbal creativity. They also propose that different forms of creative thinking require different cognitive abilities, which, in turn, help shape a preferred mode of thinking. They suggest scientists and engineers are likely to be spatial visualisers since they need to be able to mentally manipulate three-dimensional shapes and the relationships between objects.

An excellent example of this kind of thinking is to be found in Jim Dungey's account of how he arrived at an understanding of how the solar wind from the sun interacts with the earth's magnetic field (Chapman, 2016). He recounted being able to mentally visualise this interaction in his mind's eye in 3-D. Having solved this problem visually he spent the next few years working out how to describe this 3-D interaction mathematically. A few years later his creative insight was recognised as constituting a major advance in understanding solar plasma physics. There are times when great creative individuals arrive at the future before others.

In contrast with spatial visualisers, Kozhevnikov *et al.* suggest visual artists are more likely to be object visualisers in that their preference is for high definition pictorial and colourful mental images of objects and scenes. The Pre-Raphaelite artists would appear to fall into this category. Both spatial and object visualisation are seen as cognitive styles, underpinned by specific cognitive abilities. However, it would be misleading to see these as being mutually exclusive – they are best viewed as being preferred modes of thought.

On the basis of their research findings Kozhevnikov *et al.* conclude, 'visualisation abilities and styles play an important role in the corresponding creativity dimension', but add the caveat that this is not the whole answer, for 'style requires the use of some unique processing beyond ability, which is important for creativity' (p205). Although they carried out their research using undergraduates without any known specific learning differences, I see it as an important step forward for it requires that in addressing the question of whether dyslexics are more creative than neurotypicals it is necessary to think beyond the simple premise that dyslexics have good visual-spatial skills and therefore they are more creative. The emphasis of this research on cognitive style also appeals to me, as it fits neatly into the holistic perspective of the dyslexias being different ways of thinking.

Before considering what the 'unique processing' ability referred to in the article may be, it is necessary to address the question of why so many dyslexic individuals gravitate towards the creative industries. David Bailey first became famous in the 1960s for his fashion and celebrity photography and he shot many front covers for *Vogue*. He is dyslexic. Via an open online forum (www.Showstudio.com 12 February, 2003) I asked him how being dyslexic had influenced his photography and he replied 'I feel dyslexia gave me a privilege. It pushed me into being totally visual.' The word 'pushed' is very important. It is as if he had little choice. There is a report that in one school year he attended school on just 33 days. He left school at the age of fifteen. It is very clear that being an undiagnosed dyslexic at school in the 1940s was not a happy experience. This was still true in the 1960s (and still is for too many today). Benjamin Zephaniah (2015), a famous UK poet, said he 'suffered' at school and left at the age of thirteen unable to read or write. In spite of this he can be described as being a verbal creative. He holds the view that 'Having dyslexia can make you creative'. Like David Bailey, he sees dyslexia as pushing him into doing things differently, 'If you want to construct a sentence and can't find the word you are searching for, you have to think of a way to write round it' (2015).

Time and again, when I ask dyslexic individuals what was their favourite subject at secondary school, they frequently cite a practical subject such as music, design technology, sport, art or a science-based subject (including maths). Languages such as French, Spanish or German are almost never mentioned, other than in terms of how difficult it was to try to learn a foreign language. When subjects such as psychology or history are mentioned, it is often in terms of them being interesting but difficult, 'too many names, too many theories'.

From their early days at school, dyslexic individuals find some subjects much more difficult than others, so there is a natural tendency to gravitate towards those subjects that are much less demanding in terms of the reading and writing requirements, or ones they find particularly interesting. Provided a subject is one that engages and enthuses an individual, then the enjoyment and interest factors result in them working harder to succeed. For example, while reading books may be challenging, the reading of many scripts is easier and it may be possible to take drama rather than English Literature. For example, Patricia's favourite subjects at secondary school included drama, physical education and maths. After taking performing arts as one of her subjects in her last years at high school, she obtained a place at one of the UK's most prestigious acting schools. In spite of the words in a script being 'all over the place', she is one of the first of the actors to be 'off the book' in rehearsals. Being dyslexic, she has had to work harder than her peers for many years and this has enabled her to achieve her ambition of becoming an actor.

One of the key factors in being creative is hard work. When Turner died he left 19,000 watercolours, drawings and oil paintings to the British nation. When asked for advice about his success he replied, 'The only secret I have got is damned hard work' (Dunne, 2003). The size of his legacy is a clear indication of that hard work. In the current century James Dyson is internationally renowned for his innovative design, with one of his best known inventions being the world's first bagless vacuum cleaner. However, in order to reach a point where he could start producing them for sale, the design process involved creating 5,127 prototypes. Turner's comment about 'dammed hard work' is applicable. For many people with dyslexia too, huge effort and perseverance are life-long habits.

Being creative is not an instant process, but is best thought of as consisting of stages. The first stage is preparation. Richard Feynman, one of the great physicists of the twentieth century, stated you first need to know what the right question is before you search for an answer. This is part of the preparation process. This stage also requires the gathering of information. I remember talking to one fashion student who is dyslexic about her creative approach. She explained that she has created a collection of shoe boxes that are full of objects, such as swatches of fabric, buttons, lace, shells and feathers. On being presented with a design brief she would sit down with her boxes and play around with combinations of materials and objects. This could take many hours and can be viewed as a form of free association. She would also spend hours in the archives of the Victoria and Albert Museum in order to draw inspiration from the past. Also, as she was studying in London, she was constantly exposed to a wide range

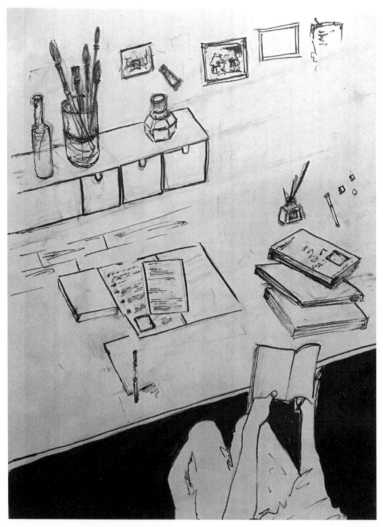

Illustration 8.1

of cultural styles. All these sources fed into her eventual design concept.

Fashion students may be given several weeks to respond to a brief. In some disciplines the preparation time lasts for years. Charles Darwin set sail in the Beagle in 1831, not returning until five years later. By visiting new worlds he was exposed to new species and cultures. Prior to that he had already read and been influenced by Charles Lyell's recently published book '*Principles of Geology*' in which Lyell suggested, controversially, geology was a process that occurred slowly. This concept, along with Darwin's previous experience of geology, enabled him to draw upon ideas and facts stored in his long-term memory. The next stage after preparation is incubation. This is the stage during which the question to be answered ticks over in the back of your mind. Darwin's big question was how to account for changes in animal characteristics over time. This was an issue he mulled over and collected evidence for over a period of many years.

The third stage is illumination. Scott Kaufman is the Science Director of the Imagination Institute (part of the University of Pennsylvania). His advice is to stop thinking about the question for a while. He claims just letting your mind wander at this stage results in greater creativity and this may well be the time when free association is important. In their 2016 paper on the '*Ten Habits of Highly Creative People*', Kaufman and Gregoire recommend 'taking a five-minute day dreaming break every hour' when working hard on a project that requires creative thinking. A classic example of how taking time out to let your mind wander results in a major creative solution is given in Charles Townes account of how he solved the question of how to achieve a beam of pure wavelength light – the basis of the laser. Charles Townes was sitting on a bench in a park in Washington DC and suddenly noticed how sunlight was being reflected off red azalea blooms. He realised he could mimic this reflection of light inside a ruby and went on to build the world's first maser – the precursor to the laser. However, when you do hit upon a solution, this is not the end of the process. You need to verify it by checking that it works and whether the evidence supports it or it fits the brief. The time between setting sail in the Beagle until publishing *On the Origin of Species* was twenty-eight years.

The careers of Turner, Darwin and Dyson are characterised by exceptional dedication. A strong commitment to hard work is also demonstrated by many dyslexic students I see. Typically, it will take them two or three times longer to write an essay than others on their course. Revision takes longer. Having to put in additional effort becomes a way of life. Being dyslexic also influences the choice of which subjects to avoid and which to pursue. I do not believe that dyslexics are born with a natural creative advantage. Rather, being dyslexic results in individuals opting for what can be seen as the path of least resistance as they proceed through school into higher education and then into employment, often in a creative industry.

The same principle applies to people with dyspraxia. The combination of poor hand-eye coordination and poor spatial awareness results in them avoiding those subjects and career paths that require these specific skills, such as fashion, catering and graphic design. However, many have considerable verbal skills and it is no surprise that Daniel Radcliffe and Florence Welch (of Florence + the Machine), who are both dyspraxic, could be described as verbal creatives. The being 'pushed' into a career path that David Bailey refers to also applies to individuals with dyspraxia and/or ADHD.

There is no doubt that people with ADHD can be highly creative – David Bowie being a classic example. But the circumstances need to be appropriate. Careers that offer an element of risk (e.g. being a stand-up comedian), require creative solutions within a short time-frame (e.g. writing adverts for radio), involve being out and about meeting people and solving problems (e.g. a transport manager) or require intense performance under pressure (e.g. an A&E specialist or a popular music performer) are the type of careers that appeal. But ADHD can pose challenges as well. If the preparation stage needs to be lengthy, procrastination will be an issue, as will verification.

A desire for perfectionism is another factor. Thomas was a student on a degree course in music composition. In his first semester he would not hand in a composition to his tutor until he was satisfied it was the best it could possibly be. His verification stage was becoming overly demanding. Fortunately, Thomas's tutor recognised this issue early on and told him, 'You have to learn to be messy'. Thomas took this on board and, to his surprise, found himself being able to come up with a new composition each week.

It is as if Thomas's tutor had enabled him to stop at the illumination stage so that his creative ideas, even if not yet fully formed, could be explored with others. Thomas gave himself permission to produce work that was not perfect and he became much more productive and willing to take chances. Freedom to be imperfect without being penalised is important.

Individuals with ADHD frequently describe themselves as being hyper-sensitive and easily distracted by sounds, movement and visual detail, but this can be used to an advantage. For example, Thomas said he often arrives at a new composition by picking up patterns in sounds, and gave as an example listening to the rain on his window one night and suddenly spotting a rhythm he could use. Kayla, who also has ADHD, is a song-writer and composer and said her creativity comes from urban landscapes, such as standing by a roundabout and listening, or from a natural activity such as the sound of hands moving over an uneven surface. Once she has 'a beat' she can work with, she creates a melody. Only then will she compose lyrics. She pointed out she is most creative when day dreaming.

For many people with ADHD, day dreaming is a normal part of life. By switching, often involuntary, into this default network mode, they enter a world of imagination. Imagination is also one of the key factors that contributes to being creative. There is a general acceptance that Roald Dahl was dyslexic. One of the last books he wrote was about a dyslexic vicar. (Visual stress may also have been present as he wrote on yellow paper.) To enjoy the worlds Roald Dahl wrote about is to enter his vivid imagination.

However, to be imaginative it is not necessary to be dyslexic or have ADHD. It is probably an almost universal human thought process. A few gifted individuals are able to use it to an exceptional degree. For J.K. Rowling, imagination is a vital element. In 2016 she said that, while it is almost a decade since her last *Harry Potter* book, 'It doesn't mean my imagination stopped … I carry that world around in my head all the time' (Crompton, 2016).

Music can also evoke imagined worlds. Nigel Kennedy, who is dyslexic, in a 2012 YouTube video of him playing Vivaldi's *Four Seasons*, describes the imagery he experiences while playing the last movement of the *Autumn* suite: 'It is about a hunt scene … you can see the hare being killed … it is pictured well in the music … at the end you see a caricature of the hunt crowd moving off'. Professional musicians don't just play music, they interpret it in an act of creativity. A pianist who has a diagnosis of ADHD told me he arrives at an interpretation of a new piece of music by painting pictures in his head. He gave as an example how, when learning to play a Bach fugue, he created a mental image of a goldfish that moved by rapid twitches. While this was an aid to developing an interpretation, he pointed out that it became a distraction during a public performance, when it was one of four things going on simultaneously in his head. Rory Bremner's comment that ADHD 'is both a blessing and a curse' also applies to this musician.

Although visualisation plays a part in how some musicians experience and interpret a piece of music, it would be wrong to assume this is a universal experience. For example, a number of musicians I have met report responding to music emotionally rather than in terms of mental imagery. While imagined visual worlds, for some, appear to be a key element of the creative process, there are other ways of expanding mental horizons. For Charles Darwin it was travelling to different countries and islands, especially the Galapagos Islands. J.M.W. Turner was also well travelled and equally as influenced by Yorkshire as by the Alps. For those working in areas such as fashion, design and music, living in a city as multi-cultural as London find that the sheer variety of everyday sights and sounds provides them with invaluable stimuli for being creative.

What should not be overlooked is that problem solving is a universal human characteristic. Every time you ask yourself a mundane question, such as which new shoes to buy, you are engaged in problem solving. You may not necessarily see this as being creative, but the process of arriving at an answer is not a linear one akin to solving an equation. It requires quite complex thinking about colour, style, material, cost and functionality. A decision may also be influenced by emotional factors such as the possible reactions of other people to your choice. It is difficult to think of any area of life that does not require creative thought.

Therefore, when considering why dyslexia is associated with being creative, the phrasing should be 'being **more** creative'. My response is that an individual's neurocognitive profile plays a vital part in shaping their preferences and choices. It so happens that many of the creative industries provide more opportunities for a dyslexic-style of thinking than many other forms of employment. Being creative requires application and dedication, and the need for dyslexics to work harder than others throughout school engenders a life-long habit which is advantageous, not just in the creative industries. However, everyone can benefit from taking steps to widen their mental horizons. While we may be partially shaped by our neurocognitive profile, we can also take active steps to assist this process in a positive way.

References

Alexander-Passe, N. (2010) (Ed). *Dyslexia and Creativity: An Investigation from Differing Perspectives*. Hauppauge, NY: Nova Science Publisher.

Chapman, S. (2016) Electrodynamics and astrophysics: Thinking in pictures. Paper presented at the international conference, The Eye's Mind: Visual Imagination, Neuroscience and the Humanities. University of East Anglia, May 21–22, 2016.

Crompton, S. (2016) Harry Potter and the Cursed Child. *The Observer*, June 5.

Dunne, A. (2003) Seeing Turner in a different light. *The Irish Times*, January 25. Available at: www.irishtimes.com/news/seeing-turner-in-a-different-light-1.346626. Last accessed June 22, 2016.

Graves, J. (2007) Dance, desire and dyslexia – Random thoughts on creativity. In Kiziewicz, M., & Biggs, I. (Eds.) *Cascade: Creativity across Science, Art, Dyslexia, Education*. University of Bath. Available at: www.bath.ac.uk/cascade/pdf/cascadefullbook.pdf. Last accessed June 24, 2016.

Kaufman, S.B. & Gregoire, C. (2016) Ten Habits of Highly Creative People. http://greatergood.berkeley.edu/article/item/ten_habits_of_highly_creative_people. Last accessed June 24, 2016.

Kennedy, N. (2012) Vivaldi: The four seasons. *YouTube*. Available at: www.youtube.com/watch?v=4JbK7k-rZ5E. Last accessed June 24, 2016.

Kozhevnikov, M., Kozhevnikov, M., Yu, C.J., & Blazhenkova, O. (2013) Creativity, visualization abilities, and visual cognitive style. *British Journal of Educational Psychology*, 83: 196–209.

Wolf, M. (2008) *Proust and the Squid: The Story and Science of the Reading Brain*. Icon Books, Cambridge.

Zephaniah, B. (2015) Young and dyslexic? You've got it going on. *The Guardian*, October 2, p35.

Websites

Rory Bremner (2014) Living with ADHD is "hell". *The BBC*. Available at: www.bbc.co.uk/news/health-29794415. Last accessed June 24, 2016.

Chapter 9

Sports and genes

In July 2011 *The Independent* newspaper had the following headline:

> Evidence grows that sport is a productive path for dyslexics.

This linking of dyslexia with sporting achievement did not come as a surprise to me. In 2008 I reported that, of the students I had diagnosed as being dyslexic, about 1 in 8 had excelled at a sporting activity in that they had been selected to represent their county, region or country in their particular sport or sports. Of those who had competed at national or international level, this was almost always in individual rather than team sports. This trend has continued as, since then, I have seen 30 individuals I assessed with dyslexia who have represented their county at a sport or sports. Six of these had also achieved at national level. Just one of these six, a Dutch student, was a member of a team sport (volleyball). The other sports were judo, cycling, triathlon, boxing and Tae-Kwon-Do.

Chris Boardman is a classic example of someone with dyslexia who has achieved at the highest level in an individual sport. He is a time trialist and won gold in the individual pursuit at the Barcelona Olympic Games. He also holds the one-hour cycling world record. Like many dyslexics he acknowledges he has 'a terrible memory generally'. However, because he has a much stronger visual than verbal memory, by riding each mountain stage of the Tour de France in advance he was able to 'picture how I'm going to ride it' (Maume, 1997). Jackie Stewart, three times Formula One World Champion, who is also dyslexic, also has a weak verbal memory but a strong visual memory: 'It has always seemed a paradox that I can't recite the alphabet beyond the letter "P", but I know every single gear change and braking distance required to negotiate the 187 corners around the 14.7 mile circuit at the old Nürburgring in Germany' (2007).

J.B. Holmes, a successful golf professional, is also able to draw upon his visual memory of a course he has played before: 'Once I get on a golf course, I can usually remember all the holes, where they placed the pins before and where my shots went' (Fleming, 2011).

There are also many examples of dyslexics being outstanding at team games. Lee Bryne represented Wales at rugby. Like Chris Boardman, he too identified verbal memory as being an issue but saw his spatial awareness as a strength, 'I would be more worried about remembering where I would have to stand than worrying about the game. But I could see space before it happened – quicker than anybody else – so in a way I suppose it was a gift for me' (2016). The neurocognitive profile for people with dyslexia is typically spiky, revealing good verbal and visual reasoning skills but weaknesses in working memory and processing speed, so it would not be surprising to find this plays a part in influencing sporting preferences. Team sports, such as netball, basketball, rugby and football, all require the mastering of often complex rules, remembering pre-game instructions and the ability to communicate with other team members while playing.

Working memory is important for all of these aspects. For example, I have met female students with dyslexia who have given up playing netball early on because they could not remember the zone rules and therefore gave away penalties, much to the annoyance of their fellow team members and their coach. Individual sports, such as athletics, or sports such as rowing are much less demanding in terms of working memory. I remember Steve Redgrave, Britain's greatest Olympian, who won five successive gold medals, talking at a British Dyslexia Association International Conference about his difficulties with remembering the rules for football when he was at primary school. He went on to say that in rowing the memory demands are minimal for you can only go in one direction. When I carried out an exploratory analysis (2008) comparing the neurocognitive profiles of male rugby players with those of male runners (cross-country and track) – all of whom had represented their county or achieved a higher level – the rugby players scored noticeably higher on working memory than the runners, while the runners scored higher than the rugby players on processing speed.

However, two caveats are necessary. The numbers for each group were small, and the average score for each group masks considerable variation. This individual variation is captured in the neurocognitive profiles of Anna and Charlotte. Both have represented their county at hockey and both have very good verbal and visual reasoning skills. However, while Anna's processing speed score is in the bottom 30 per cent, Charlotte's score for processing speed places her in the top 39 per cent. In contrast, Charlotte's working memory score is in the bottom 23 per cent, with Anna scoring higher – a midpoint score of 50. In terms of their working memory and processing speed abilities they are the opposite of each other. However, although Charlotte is better than Anna at remembering information for a short period of time, her ability to remember is still well below expectation. As a working memory weakness can be viewed as an obstacle to be overcome rather than an advantage in sports, it is necessary to consider those factors that might enhance sporting performance.

Could visualisation be one of those factors? Fleming (2011) refers to dyslexic elite sports performers talking 'of having an advantage in terms of visualisation, spatial awareness, creativity and memory'. Driskell *et al.* posed that question in 1994, and concluded that mental practice (which includes visualisation) can have 'a positive and significant effect on performance' (p481). However, there are reasons for questioning the belief that visualisation is a typical dyslexic strength (see Chapter 6). On examining the self-ratings of strength of visualisation when reading for those dyslexic athletes who have reached county level or higher, the number who can be categorised as strong visualisers (43 per cent) is no different from that found for dyslexics in general. However, of the small number who had reached a national level, 80 per cent were strong visualisers. These figures can only be viewed as indicative, rather than as providing robust evidence. While it is recognised that the use of visualisation can be a useful training technique for sporting skills, and is now included in the training programme of many sports, from rugby to high jump, I am not yet convinced that being dyslexic brings with it an advantage in being naturally strong at visualisation. It may be that those who are strong at visualisation gravitate towards those activities where visualisation is beneficial.

Motivation also plays a part. Ben Youngs (2015), who at the time of writing is a member of the England rugby team, saw sport as being 'an escape route' for himself when he was at school. (NB: It can also provide a means of working off frustration – see Illustration 9.1.) Standing in class having to read aloud was a nightmare experience for Ben, as it is for many dyslexics, but on the rugby pitch his sporting ability provides him with a means of expressing how good he can be in a non-academic environment. If it is the case that dyslexic individuals have a greater potential to do well at sports, is it then, as Ben Youngs suggests, because for them sport is an escape from the classroom? I have encountered a similar comment with regard to art classes at school, in that in art lessons you don't have to read or write essays. Art at school may provide a temporary escape from those subjects that require good literacy skills, but it does not automatically mean you will be good at art, even if it is a subject you enjoy.

Illustration 9.1

While I accept there is an element of truth in Ben Youngs' comment, I don't think it is quite so simple. For example, Ben Youngs broke his school record for the 200 metres, a record that had stood for twenty-five years. It is clear that, physiologically, he is exceptional, and sport provided him with an opportunity to choose a career that is free of the kind of demands dyslexic individuals find challenging. The question therefore becomes one of whether being dyslexic confers some form of physiological advantage.

Before examining this a little more closely, there is another factor to consider – application. In 1976 Bruce Jenner became, for a time, one of the most famous athletes, winning gold for the decathlon at the Montreal Olympics (and also beginning the practice of waving the national flag on winning). The decathlon consists of ten individual athletic events. He attributed his win to being dyslexic in that 'If I had been a better reader, then that would have come easily, sports would have come easily … and I never would have realised that the way you get ahead in life is hard work'. After coming tenth at the previous Olympics, Jenner said he trained every day for six to eight hours for the next four years.

Application and dedication are vital for sporting achievement, but, once again, this cannot be the whole story. Having seen many athletes put in hours of training but not succeed in winning, I accept that application, in and of itself, is not sufficient. There has to be an extra element as well. For individuals with ADHD there are two factors that act as barriers to the hard work that is required to develop sporting skills: a low boredom threshold and

a quest for perfectionism. It is not unusual for someone
with ADHD who loves sport to have engaged with a wide
range of sporting activities. For example, Angus said he has
always enjoyed taking part in sports, including rugby, judo,
hockey and golf. He preferred team sports as 'everything
is always changing every minute'. Angus would take up
a new sport with enthusiasm and often make good initial
progress. However, once he reached a level where more
sustained effort was needed to improve and progress, he
would move on to a new activity, as the hours of practice
now became boring. In addition, as a perfectionist, he was
dispirited by how long it would take him to reach the level
he desired, and this also contributed to his decision to
switch to yet another sport.

For someone who has the combined form of ADHD
(attentional difficulties combined with restlessness and
impulsivity) sport offers a legitimate way of running off
excess energy. Angus described himself as being 'an engine
in shoes'. Like many others with ADHD, he has found
taking part in physical exercise results, for a time, in his
mind feeling calmer. Greg LeMond has won the Tour de
France three times. He also has ADHD. His comment:
'Exercise opened my brain to learning; it has to be more
than walking though. It has to be something with some
intensity when your heart rate is really high', captures
this experience of physical exercise resulting in the brain
temporarily slowing down from racing mode.

This improvement in focus when taking part in sports
is often mentioned by people with ADHD. Mustafa has
ADHD and he has represented his county at both cricket

(as a bowler) and football. When taking part in a sport he is hyper-focused, 'When I am engaged in sports I am better focused than in anything else'. For some ADHD individuals an element of risk is vital for maintaining concentration, so the kind of sport undertaken is a crucial choice. Jade represented her county at cricket. When she was fielding her attention span was poor. However, when given the opportunity to be wicket keeper her focus was sharp. Because wicket keepers run a risk of being hurt, this element of danger resulted in her becoming hyper-focused.

Professional cyclists, when racing in a group in close proximity to each other, need to be fully focused at all times. Professional cycling is also a high risk sport. Balzac was good enough at cycling to become a member of his national junior squad. However, he quickly earned the nickname *Hazard* due to his propensity to cause crashes. A momentary lapse of focus has serious consequences in professional cycling, and he quit the sport before he was twenty. Some individuals develop techniques to help them maintain focus. Jamie was a goalkeeper and played football at a semi-professional level. Because he was very prone to losing focus in the last ten minutes of a match he took to shouting instructions to his team members to help him maintain focus.

When ADHD is present it is frequently accompanied by another specific learning difference. About 30 per cent of the ADHD individuals I see are also dyspraxic and about 20 per cent dyslexic. I have yet to meet anyone with the combination of ADHD and dyspraxia who has taken part in sport at county level. This is not surprising. However, of those with both ADHD and dyslexia, the number who have succeeded at a high level of sporting performance is at least twice as many as anticipated, for there were slightly more ADHD individuals with dyslexia than without in the group for whom I have data. This carries the implication that being dyslexic conveys a slight sporting advantage even when ADHD is present.

None of the current theories of dyslexia can account for this, and one, the cerebellar deficit hypothesis, suggests the opposite may be true. Visual information within the brain is handled by two main nerve pathways, the parvocellular and the magnocellular pathway. The magnocellular pathway is the main one for processing rapid visual changes and it has been proposed that a deficit in this pathway underlies the difficulties dyslexics experience when scanning text. Nicolson *et al.* (2001) go further than just focusing on reading and spelling, for they propose that such a deficit also impedes both the speed at which a skill is learnt (skill automatization) and balance. In a separate paper Angela Fawcett and Roderick Nicolson (2001), conclude 'it is difficult for dyslexic children to become expert in any skill, whether cognitive or motor. Consequently, they will suffer problems in fluency for any skill that should become automatic via extensive practice' (p92).

The cerebellar deficit hypothesis is not without its critics. My opinion is that it cannot be applied universally to dyslexia, for I have seen significant numbers of dyslexics who have excellent sports skills, not just those who have achieved a county level of performance. Of the most recent dyslexics I have seen who have performed at county level,

30 per cent played either hockey, lacrosse or camogie (a female version of the Irish game of hurling). These sports require really good hand-eye coordination and fast reaction times. They also need excellent balance. Other sports, including basketball, cycling, kayaking, football and rugby, also require good motor coordination and balance. The achievement record of these individuals is incompatible with the central premise of the cerebral deficit hypothesis.

If it is the case that being dyslexic confers a sporting advantage, how can this be accounted for? To be successful at a high level requires strong commitment and there is an argument that being dyslexic leads individuals to learn to work harder (the same argument I use in Chapter 8 on being creative). Motivation is also important and the thrill of being very good at an activity valued by others will be a powerful spur to continuing with that activity, as well as a major boost to self-esteem. This factor may help explain why, when dyspraxia is present, many more males than females report bouts of depression (Grant, 2014). Self-esteem in males is more closely bound up with being good at physical activities, such as sports. For people with dyspraxia, this means of gaining social approval from peers is absent and this in turn impacts negatively on the development of self-worth.

When dyspraxia is present, motor coordination can be improved through taking part in sports and dance. Corina's birth was two months before the due date and she suffered a cerebral haemorrhage soon after her first birthday, which resulted in major difficulties in learning to walk. Her hand-eye coordination was also quite poor. (NB: Her dyspraxia is probably an acquired one.) Corina's parents were very keen to help improve her coordination and, in addition to spending time each day engaged in physiotherapy exercises, they also enrolled her in a number of physical activity sessions. She attended ballet lessons from the age of four to seven and then took up gym. She has also learnt to ski, swim, and play badminton. Although her speed of learning was slow in each case, she nevertheless achieved a reasonable level of performance in a variety of activities, such as the back stroke in swimming. However, in spite of the massive effort she had made over many years she experienced bullying in physical education classes at secondary school. Her huge application was offset by the bullying and this had a negative impact on her motivation to continue with physical education lessons as well as on her self-esteem.

When I met Sigrid she was training to be a singer at a music conservatoire. Like many dyspraxics her birth was a difficult one and forceps-assisted. When asked about her sporting abilities she replied she was not good at basketball as she 'couldn't dribble the ball'. To help improve her coordination and balance Sigrid attended ballet classes from the age of three until she was about eleven, when she switched to jazz dance. She felt dance lessons helped to improve her coordination. As a consequence, she is comfortable with performing in public. Sigrid said she is 'not that slow' at learning new dance routines, as long as she remembers a series of steps in short sequences, which she then links together.

There is evidence that some individuals with dyspraxia can achieve a high level of physical performance in spite of poor motor coordination. Interviews with dyspraxic contemporary dance students (Wilkinson *et al.*, 2008) at Trinity Laban Conservatoire of Music and Dance revealed that, through dance, their improvements in muscular strength and posture contribute to an enhancement in self-image. By choosing contemporary dance over ballet they could escape the strict regimentation of ballet training and focus more on improvisation. This emphasis on routine is an issue for dancers with ADHD. Jeremy was, at various times, a member of the English National Ballet and the Spanish National Ballet. He was also the principal dancer in a West End musical but left after six months as his boredom threshold is low and having to perform the same routine night after night resulted in him feeling frustrated.

There are many factors that contribute to sporting and dance achievement. For dyspraxics, the challenges can appear daunting, and they are, but a few do manage to surmount them. For individuals with ADHD who have high levels of energy, this would appear to be an advantageous factor, but issues of boredom and perfectionism can be the downside. For dyslexics, issues of working memory and processing speed may make them relatively slow at learning, but the success rate appears to be high.

In accounting for such success it is necessary to move beyond the available evidence and engage in speculative thinking by taking an evolutionary perspective. There is a considerable body of evidence that both dyslexia and ADHD are found across many different cultures and that they are inherited, more so with ADHD than dyslexia. The first written account of ADHD dates from 1796, and dyslexia from 1875. In spite of both appearing to be relatively recent discoveries, the fact that both are present on a world-wide basis and both have a genetic element can only be accounted for by their being, in evolutionary terms, ancient behavioural features, probably dating from the time of the great human migration out of East Africa about 60,000 to 70,000 years ago. This implies that both ADHD and dyslexia provided some form of evolutionary advantage.

In the case of ADHD, it could be argued that the high level of restlessness and need for new experiences played a significant role in enabling humans to seek out new lands. There is also an argument that in a nomadic society, where the need to be continually foraging for food, taking advantage of opportunities and constantly scanning the environment for threats (this is where hyper-sensitivity is an advantage), people with ADHD might have an advantage. Eisenberg and Campbell (2011) refer to one study from Kenya that has found an association between the presence of a gene linked with dopamine production and better eating in members of a tribe who were still nomadic, compared with members of that culture with the same gene who had settled in one place and were less well nourished. (NB: Dopamine is a neurotransmitter linked to ADHD. As dopamine production increases attention improves.) The finding, reported in Chapter 6, that ADHD individuals are, in general, more visual thinkers than neurotypicals would also have been an advantage in pre-literate societies.

The literature linking dyslexia with evolutionary advance is almost non-existent. Even in pre-literate societies it can be argued that a weakness in working memory and a slow processing speed could still have been a disadvantage. However, if there is a loose link between dyslexia and sporting ability, it is easy to understand how this would have been an advantage in societies where endurance, strength and skill would have been important for hunting or fighting. Such males would have been the more dominant members of their culture and often had more female partners, thus securing a wider dispersion of the genes associated with dyslexia. It may be no coincidence that several current members of royal families are known to be dyslexic, including Sweden's Princess Victoria and Prince Carl Philip, and Princess Beatrice in the UK: 'School was a nightmare. I struggled … My earliest memory is trying to read Beatrix Potter and the words were literally jumping off the page' (Coughlan, 2016). One news item (Sinha, 2015) refers to the Prince Carl Philip's love of sports, including Formula One, hunting and other outdoor pursuits. I know of members of a Middle Eastern royal family who are also dyslexic. Dyslexia is not just a European characteristic.

In 2008 I reported finding that the incidence of birthing complications was very low for dyslexics who had achieved at a high level in sport. The data I have gathered since then continues to support this observation. In contrast, at least 50 per cent of the dyspraxic individuals I have seen have a history of birthing difficulties. It is possible that, until recent times, dyslexic individuals who held a position of power in their society had better access than most to both good nutrition and good health care, including midwifery. This would have helped ensure more children would survive and thus strengthen genetic inheritance.

Being dyslexic, dyspraxic or having ADHD influences so many facets of everyday life, including enjoyment and aptitude for sports and dance. While it is possible to identify some common factors, we are still a long way from real understanding. Hence the high degree of speculative thinking in this chapter.

References

Byrne, L. (2016) Dyslexia and me: Rugby star Byrne on life with the learning difficulty. *ITV Report*, March 14, 2016 at 6:15am.

Coughlan, S. (2016) Princess Beatrice urges young to speak up for themselves. Available at: http://www.bbc.co.uk/news/education-36539952. Last accessed June 16, 2016.

Driskell, J.E., Copper, C., & Moran, A. (1994) Does mental practice enhance performance? *Journal of Applied Psychology*, 79: 481–492.

Eisenberg, D., and Campbell, B. (2011) The evolution of ADHD: Social context matters. *Medicine for Life*, 20 October.

Fawcett, A.J., & Nicolson, R.I. (2001) Dyslexia: The role of the cerebellum. In Fawcett, A. (Ed), *Dyslexia: Theory & Good Practice*, Whurr Publishing, London.

Fleming, M. (2011). Evidence grows that sport is a productive path for dyslexics. *The Independent*, July 20.

Grant, D.W. (2008) Sporting preferences and achievements of dyslexic and dyspraxic sports men and women: Lesson for London 2012? *Dyslexia Review*, 20: 31–37.

Grant, D.W. (2014) Specific learning difficulties. Invited paper presented at the UKAAN 4th Congress – Mind, Brain and Body, London, September 11.

Maume, C. (1997) Cycling: Riding through the ranks. Chris Boardman interviewed. *The Independent*, June 29.

Nicolson, R.I., Fawcett, A.J., & Dean, P. (2001) Developmental dyslexia: The cerebellar deficit hypothesis. *Trends in Neurosciences*, 24 (9): 508–511.

Sinha, B.P. (2015) Prince Carl Philip of Sweden talks being dyslexic: His struggle with reading and writing. *International Business Times*, 17 December.

Stewart, J. (2007) Dyslexia blighted my life, *The Telegraph*, October 1.

Youngs, B. (2015) Ben Youngs reveals rugby helped tackle dyslexia. *The Daily Mail*, August 30. Available at: www.dailymail.co.uk/sport/rugbyunion/article-3216322. Last accessed August 12, 2016.

Wilkinson, J., Quin, E., Hitchins, J., Ehrenberg, S., Irvine, S., Redding, E., Bothma, H., & Pestano, C. (2008). *Report from Phase I of the Trinity Laban TQEF Funded Project on Dyspraxia in Music & Dance Students*. Trinity Laban Internal Publication, London.

Chapter 10

Invisible girls, invisible women

In 2006 Dray and her colleagues posed the question 'Why are girls with ADHD invisible?'. The same question was asked a few years later by Myttas (2009), and it is still a pressing issue. In my diagnostic practice I see equal numbers of males and females with ADHD. This is in sharp contrast to the ratios reported by clinicians who see children referred for diagnosis for suspected ADHD. Although the male/female ratio varies significantly across countries and surveys, with typical figures being somewhere between 6:1 and 12:1 (Myttas, 2009), they all report much higher numbers of males than females. Given that Cooper and O'Regan, as long ago as 2001, reported more or less equal numbers in secondary school of boys and girls having ADHD, this suggests a very high proportion of girls not having their ADHD recognised. This is important because of the high numbers of females with ADHD reporting mental health issues, such as eating disorders and high levels of anxiety and depression (Biederman *et al.*, 2010).

The widely held belief that ADHD is the province of naughty boys can, in itself, result in girls being reluctant to seek a diagnosis because they assume they cannot have

ADHD. There is some evidence that the form of ADHD that is a combination of both inattentive behaviour and hyperactivity/impulsivity is more common in boys than girls, with the consequential disruptive behaviour at home and school being very obvious and making a diagnosis more likely. However, if girls with this combined form of ADHD spend time outside engaging in physical activities, such as climbing trees and playing football, they may just be perceived as being tomboys, with the consequence that they are less likely to be referred for diagnosis.

There is a consensus that the inattentive form of ADHD (i.e. problems with attention but not hyperactivity or impulsivity) is the more difficult one to observe and diagnose. About 50 per cent of ADHD individuals have this form. In my experience, it is not until an individual with this type of ADHD is either nearing the end of high school or is at university/college that help is first requested. I suspect this is particularly true when the student is intellectually very capable and they have been able to mask their difficulties for some time, but often at a high cost to their social life and self-esteem. This is captured in a mother's email to me. She described her daughter, Harriet, as being 'a very outgoing, bubbly, happy and social child' during her primary school years. However, when she was about fourteen she started to become self-absorbed, insular and 'happy to hide away'. Initially, her mother attributed this to Harriet being a typical teenager, but she became increasingly concerned as Harriet's self-confidence ebbed away and her circle of friends grew smaller. She mentioned Harriet often experienced rapid mood changes, such as quickly becoming angry or giving vent to frustration.

During her mid- to late-teenage years Harriet had become 'invisible'. Her undiagnosed ADHD resulted in her experiencing increasing academic difficulties and she started to fall behind her friends in her ability to produce well organised work on time. She responded to these difficulties in a gender-specific manner by doing all she could to avoid drawing attention to herself. I am not alone making this observation. Myttas (2009) describes girls with the inattentive form of ADHD as often being 'academically withdrawn, shy, timid and easily overwhelmed [...] They are often more conscientious and guilt-ridden, working harder to hide academic difficulties and conform to expectations' (p8). Very occasionally, I come across a female student who will describe herself as becoming 'the clown of the class' as a means of distracting attention from her learning difficulties, but this is more usually a tactic adopted by boys. Looking back through my records, four times as many males as females describe themselves as being the 'class clown'.

Lawrence is a classic example. His mother described him as following 'the classic route of being the class clown' and as reveling in his 'undeserved reputation as 'ard'. One of his teachers remarked that in forty years of teaching, Laurence was 'the only child who had defeated' her. He had to change secondary school after two years due to frequently getting into trouble. It was not until Lawrence was in his mid-thirties that he was formally diagnosed as having the combined form of ADHD.

As even Lawrence's ADHD was not recognised until later on, it is easy to see how it is yet more difficult for girls and women to have their ADHD recognised, given that ADHD is perceived as being primarily a male characteristic and their tendency to fade into the background. It is not at all unusual for females with ADHD to report experiencing their first bout of depression in their mid- to late-teens and to be prescribed anti-depressive medication, without any steps being taken to ascertain whether the underlying factor might be undiagnosed ADHD.

It is not just ADHD that is often believed to be found primarily in males – it applies to dyslexia as well. As with ADHD, this misapprehension results in a lack of early recognition of the learning difficulties dyslexic girls experience. For example, a survey in 1990 by Shaywitz and colleagues found schools in Connecticut referred many more boys (13.6 per cent) than girls (3.2 per cent) for reading difficulties. That is a ratio of about four boys to every girl. However, a research-based approach revealed very different figures – 8.7 per cent vs 6.9 per cent – which illustrates very clearly that referrals based on the judgements of teachers were significantly influenced by gender stereotyping. This is a well known phenomenon. In spite of more recent studies demonstrating no significant differences in the frequency of reading difficulties between boys and girls (e.g. Siegel & Smythe, 2005), it is disappointing to find researchers still subscribing to the gender stereotype. For example, Fisher and her colleagues (2015) claim dyslexia 'appears to primarily affect men who are four times more likely than women to meet criteria for diagnosis' (p350).

For some years now I have assessed more women than men for dyslexia, and this may be the result of there being more females than males with undiagnosed dyslexia. For example, Eloise was eighteen when I saw her. In spite of a long history of disliking having to read aloud in class because she stumbled over words, and getting her lowest grades in language exams, it was not until she was in her last year at high school that it was finally recognised that she had a problem. Eloise's school reports described her as being 'quiet in class', and hardworking. Like many females with undiagnosed dyslexia she had decided to take care to avoid drawing attention to herself, and by being hardworking she had helped mask her difficulties. However, it is not inevitable that a girl with dyslexia will slip quietly into the background. Claudia attended a primary school that gave pupils a book each week to take home to read. When given hers, Claudia would throw a tantrum and throw the book away. She was diagnosed as being dyslexic when she was seven.

The same referral bias also applies with dyspraxia. Missiuna et al. (2006) cite studies reporting male/female ratios as varying between 3:1 and 5:1 for teacher-referred children, whereas a longitudinal survey of over 7,000 children reported a ratio of 1.7 to 1 (Lingam et al., 2009). Two reasons are given for the greater number of boys than girls being referred by teachers, including the familiar one of believing boys are more likely than girls to be dyspraxic. It is also suggested that as the co-occurrence of ADHD with dyspraxia is quite high, this also results in boys being more likely to draw attention to themselves.

Illustration 10.1

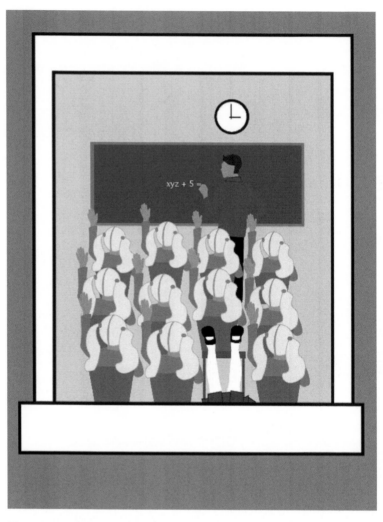

Illustration 10.2

Stereotyping is an issue. It was not until Kerry was an undergraduate that she was diagnosed as being dyspraxic and having ADHD. This was in spite of her clumsiness and restlessness being quite obvious in class at primary school. (See Illustration 10.2). She would lose concentration, fidget in her chair, and – occasionally – fall over. Typically, this was treated as Kerry being naughty by her teacher. In her illustration she has drawn the other girls as being different from herself, to capture her feelings of 'being left out and different'. If her teachers had been trained to recognise the signs of these specific learning differences, including the fact they are not more typical of males than females, Kerry's experience of school could have been very different. And so could the school days of many individuals I have seen.

References

Biederman, J., Petty, C.R., Monuteaux, M.C., Fried, R., Byrne, D., Mirto, T., Spencer, T., Wilens, T.E., & Faraone, S.V. (2010) Adult psychiatric outcomes of girls with attention deficit hyperactivity disorder: 11-year follow-up in a longitudinal case-control study. *American Journal of Psychiatry*, 167 (4): 409–417. doi: 10.1176/appi.ajp.2009.09050736. Last accessed August 12, 2016.

Cooper, P., and O'Regan, F.J. (2001) *Educating Children with AD/HD: A Teacher's Manual.* Routledge Falmer, London.

Dray, M., Campbell, M.A., & Gilmore, L.A. (2006) Why are girls with ADHD invisible? *Connections*, 23(2): 2–7, Queensland Guidance and Counselling Association Inc., Queensland.

Fisher, C., Chekaluk, E., & Irwin, J. (2015) Impaired driving performance as evidence of a magnocellular deficit in dyslexia and visual stress. *Dyslexia*, 21: 350–360.

Lingam, R., Hunt, L., Golding, J., Jongmans, M., & Emond, A. (2009) Prevalence of developmental coordination disorder using the DSM-IV at 7 years of age: A UK population–based study. *Pediatrics*, 123 (4): e693–700.

Shaywitz, S.E., Shaywitz, B.A., Fletcher, J.M., & Escobar, M.D. (1990) Prevalence of reading disability in boys and girls: Results of the Connecticut Longitudinal Study. *Journal of the American Medical Association*, 264 (8): 998–1002.

Siegel, L.S., & Smythe, I.S. (2005) Reflections on research on reading disability with special attention to gender issues. *Journal of Learning Disabilities*, 38 (5): 473–477.

Missiuna, C., Gaines, R., Soucie, H., and McLean, J. (2006) Parental questions about developmental coordination disorder: A synopsis of current evidence. *Paediatric Child Health*, 11(8): 507–512.

Myttas, N. (2009) Gender disparities: Adolescent girls with ADHD, *ADHD in Practice*. 1 (4): 8–11.

Chapter 11

Sleep

The day following her diagnosis of ADHD Kim emailed me a simple message, 'That igloo thing worked'. In common with the vast majority of people with ADHD that I meet, Kim said she has problems falling asleep at night. Even when she is physically tired, falling asleep is often very difficult because of all the thoughts she has racing around in her mind. Consequently, she tends not to go to bed until the early hours of the morning, but this is a problem when having to get up early for work or morning lectures. Difficulty with falling asleep is a well known issue for people with ADHD (e.g. Brown & McMullen 2001). A recent study of electrical brain activity while sleeping was carried out with children, half of whom had ADHD (Virring *et al.*, 2016). It found the ADHD children slept less well as it took them longer to fall asleep. Their sleep differed in other ways as well.

ADHD children, irrespective of which form of ADHD they had, were reported as experiencing more rapid eye movement (REM) sleep and more sleep cycles. REM sleep is a time when the brain is most active and vivid dreams occur. At the same time, heart beat and pace of breathing quicken. REM sleep occurs a number of times throughout the night and, in general, about 25 per cent to 30 per cent of sleeping time is in REM sleep.

It is well established that lack of sleep interferes with memory, but the big questions of why sleep is important and how it is connected with memory processes are still to be answered. However, in recent years, research has provided increasing support for the idea that sleep is essential for helping to consolidate memories. During our waking hours, memory traces are formed, but because these are new they are fragile and can be easily disrupted. While we are asleep there is much less external information coming into the brain to be processed and this significantly reduces the risk of the newly created memory traces being disrupted. It appears that the brain then switches to actively processing recent memory traces, which requires changing into a more stable state. Part of this consolidation process involves moving the new memories to different areas of the brain (e.g. Rasch & Born, 2013) and linking them up with other relevant memories. Evidence suggests this consolidation process occurs when the sleeping brain is in its most active stage, i.e. during REM sleep. If it is the case that REM sleep is important in laying down more permanent memories, why do people with ADHD experience more REM sleep?

I suspect the answer may relate to the way the ADHD brain works. When an ADHD person is awake, they describe themselves as experiencing a number of thoughts concurrently, which quickly flit in and out of consciousness. Frequently these thoughts are multi-sensory in that they consist of a combination of verbal, visual and emotional aspects. This is a form of mental hyperactivity and results in difficulties with falling asleep. It is as if the brain is in racing mode and cannot be switched off (see Illustration 11.1). During sleep there is no reason to suspect this mental hyperactivity ceases, so when REM sleep occurs the retrieval and consolidation of stored memory traces from the day's events and experiences will also be conducted in the same manner. It may also be a more complex process given the way the mind of an ADHD individual flits quickly from one thought to another. The process of sorting through recent memory traces, consolidating them and aligning them with more permanent memory systems will require more time. If it is the case that this consolidation process is also accompanied by a deletion of memory traces that are no longer needed, once again the process will be more complex, since individuals with ADHD often report difficulties with prioritising.

So where does 'the igloo thing' fit into this? Kim had reported finding it 'so, so hard' to fall asleep. Her assessment had revealed she was a very visual person, so I told her about a technique that another ADHD student with strong visualisation abilities had described to me. He imagined himself lying on his back in a field. Although he had lots of images and thoughts racing through his mind, he imagined himself creating an igloo around himself using black blocks. Once he finished this, he succeeded in blocking everything else out of his mind and then fell asleep. This also worked for Kim the first time she tried it.

Difficulties with falling asleep are also reported by about 90 per cent of people with dyslexia or dyspraxia. Many

Illustration 11.1

people find the time between trying to get to sleep and finally falling asleep is one in which ideas occur randomly, 'Falling asleep is so hard. The minute I close my eyes my brain switches on'. Frequently these pre-sleep thoughts fall into two categories: thoughts about the day just ending and thoughts about the day to follow. One feature common to most individuals with a specific learning difference is a working memory weakness. This means memories of what has been said and done during the day will be fragmented and chaotic, so part of pre-sleep time is given over to making sense of these: 'Why did I say that?', 'Should I refer to Tanner's work in my poster?', 'Was it Thursday or Friday I said I was going to meet up with Ahmed?'.

This sorting through of the day's events and planning for the next day may result in the emergence of new ideas or recalling something that should have been done but wasn't. Some people keep a notebook by their bed (see Illustration 11.2), make use of post-it notes or use their mobile phone as a recorder, because they are aware if they do not make a note of things to do or solutions to problems, they will have forgotten them by the morning. For some, this pre-sleep period can be a creative time; for others, it can be a frustrating one because it is as if ideas appear from nowhere and then disappear quickly. The poem that Sue wrote for me captures this transient state well:

> As I lie awake in bed,
> Poems come floating through my head.
> I try to grasp them, grab them, catch them,
> But somehow I just can't nab them.

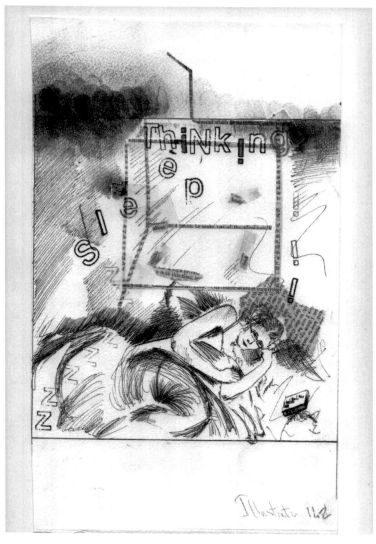

Illustration 11.2

As far as I am aware, there have been no studies of the electrical activity of the brains of dyslexic and dyspraxic individuals during sleep, so we don't know whether their sleep patterns are more like ADHD individuals or neurotypicals. However, it would not surprise me if it is more typical of ADHD, given the role REM sleep plays in consolidating memory traces. As REM is associated with vivid dreams, and many individuals with dyspraxia or dyslexia have very strong visual memory, it would also not be surprising if REM sleep is particularly important for the consolidation of visual memories. If there is a difference between the pre-sleep and sleep experiences of ADHD individuals and those who are dyslexic or dyspraxic, it is likely to involve agitation of thought processes. This can be seen by comparing the two illustrations in this chapter. The first, drawn by an ADHD student who is also dyspraxic, reflects an agitated state of mind, whereas the second, drawn by a dyslexic illustrator, reflects a calmer state of mind.

Given that so many individuals with specific learning differences report sleep difficulties, with, in my experience, ADHD individuals being particularly badly affected, are there ways of minimising this? I've put this question to a number of people and the only common theme of their responses is giving the mind something neutral to focus on. For example, Megan said she usually plays an audio book she has listened to many times before to help her fall asleep; Paul said by taking up yoga and becoming a practising Buddhist he has learnt to use meditation as a calming influence; Nitin always needs something playing in the background, such as a DVD, otherwise he finds it difficult to fall asleep. And then there is 'the igloo thing'.

References

Brown, T.E., & McMullen, W.J. (2001) Attention deficit disorders and sleep/arousal disturbance. *Annals of the New York Academy of Sciences*, 931: 271–286.

Rasch, B., & Born, J. (2013) About sleep's role in memory. *Physiological Reviews*, 93 (2): 681–766.

Virring, A, Lambek, R., Thomsen, P.H., Møller, L.R., & Jennum, P.J. (2016) Disturbed sleep in attention-deficit hyperactivity disorder (ADHD) is not a question of psychiatric comorbidity or ADHD presentation. *Journal of Sleep Research*, 25 (3): 333–40, doi: 10.1111/jsr.12377.

Chapter 12

Neurodiversity and concluding remarks

On May 13, 2016, John McDonnell, Labour Member of Parliament and Shadow Chancellor, tweeted: 'I am supporting calls for Labour to develop an Autism Manifesto and appoint a Shadow Minister for Neurodiversity & will consult on details.'

Even though I suspect we are a long way from this proposal becoming a reality, the fact it has been made at all represents a major step forward, especially as the term 'neurodiversity' is a recent one, probably having been used first in 1998 by Singer as a positive way of referring to individuals with autism. Within a short time it began to be adopted as a positive way of stating that the brains of individuals with specific learning differences (including dyslexia, dyspraxia and ADHD) are wired differently from those of most other people (neurotypicals). The adoption of the term 'neurodiversity' can be seen as a commitment to a social model of disability, for when it is used it announces:we 'Yes, I am different, but I want to be accepted for who I am, not what society would like me to be'. It also implies that the neurotypical society should implement changes to accommodate and respect specific learning differences rather than to seek cures for them. The social model of disability is a rejection of the medical model, with its reliance on terms such as 'dysfunction', 'disorder', 'symptoms' and 'co-morbidity'. Roddy Slorach (2016) sums this approach up neatly with his comment that neurodiversity differences 'should be recognised as natural human variation instead of being pathologised' (p212).

There are two consistent themes running throughout this book: individuality and commonality. These are not contradictory, but rather complementary aspects of understanding how variations in fundamental cognitive processes colour and shape the everyday behaviours and experiences of individuals with specific learning differences. Because the cognitive profile of strengths and weaknesses varies from one person to another, diagnostic categories are imperfect since they imply uniformity and clear-cut boundaries. The reality is very different. It is these elements of individuality and blurring of boundaries that have led a number of individuals with specific learning differences to prefer the description of being neurodiverse.

The use of the phrase 'specific learning difference' instead of 'specific learning difficulty' has been adopted specifically to reflect the fact that there are many different ways of learning. In historical and evolutionary terms, the newness of having to learn and work mainly through reading and writing rather than through listening, seeing and doing has resulted in significant numbers of individuals being disadvantaged. Symbolic writing was first developed about 3,000 years ago as wedge-shapes on clay tablets (cuneiform script) and alphabetic writing became established around the time of the Romans. However, it was not until the introduction of universal compulsory primary education in 1870 in the UK that it became necessary for every child to learn skills of reading, writing and spelling.

Millennia living as hunters and gathers did not prepare the human brain for the cognitive skills required for reading. It is a requirement imposed on pre-existing neurological systems and pathways. This imposition is why Andrew Ellis (1985) said 'Whatever dyslexia turns out to be, it is not a reading disorder'. It is a tribute to the plasticity of the human brain that the skill of reading is mastered by so many. We have evolved to explore and deal creatively with changes beyond our control (such as weather, the availability of food, sickness, danger, etc.), an environment which arguably best suits the ADHD brain. If it is the case that, for some, being dyslexic is linked with physical prowess, this would also have been advantageous. Variations in the human genome give rise to individual differences and confer evolutionary advantage. Neurodiversity is a positive way of acknowledging this.

In order to know how to improve the everyday experiences of the neurodiverse in a world geared to the neurotypical, it is first necessary to understand the cognitive and sensory worlds of the neurodiverse. Those worlds, explored in this book, are undoubtedly complex, complicated and very varied. Through understanding comes acceptance. Through understanding comes positivity. This is captured well in Kerry's email to me following her diagnosis of ADHD:

Such self-awareness is going to help me achieve what I aspire to do in the future, although it will take a great deal of self-discipline, organisation and research. I feel ready for this now.

References

Ellis, A. (1985) The production of spoken words: A cognitive neuropsychological perspective. In A.W. Ellis (Ed.), *Progress in the Psychology of Language*, Vol 2. Erlbaum, Hillsdale, NJ.

Slorach, R. (2016) *A Very Capitalist Condition: A History and Politics of Disability*. Bookmark Publications, London.

Singer, J. (1998) Odd people in: The birth of community amongst people on the autistic spectrum: A personal exploration of a new social movement based on neurological diversity, Honours dissertation, University of Technology, Sydney.

Further reading

Pollak, D. (2009) *Neurodiversity in Higher Education: Positive Responses to Specific Learning Differences*, Wiley-Blackwell, West Sussex.